**JUSTIN
BIEBER**

JUSTIN BIEBER

S A R A H   O L I V E R

JB

JOHN BLAKE

Published by John Blake Publishing Ltd,
3 Bramber Court, 2 Bramber Road,
London W14 9PB, England

www.johnblakepublishing.co.uk

www.facebook.com/Johnblakepub

twitter.com/johnblakepub

First published in paperback in 2011

ISBN: 978 1 84358 379 0

British Library Cataloguing-in-Publication Data:

A catalogue record for this book is available from the British Library.

Design by www.envydesign.co.uk

Printed and bound by CPI Group (UK) Ltd, Croydon, CR0 4YY

3 5 7 9 10 8 6 4 2

Papers used by John Blake Publishing are natural, recyclable products
made from wood grown in sustainable forests. The manufacturing processes
conform to the environmental regulations of the country of origin.

Every attempt has been made to contact the relevant copyright-holders,
but some were unobtainable. We would be grateful if the
appropriate people could contact us.

Other A–Z books by Sarah Oliver:

Dedicated with love to Dan,
the best brother in the world.

INTRODUCTION

The Justin Bieber A–Z is jam-packed with everything you need to know about the biggest star on the planet. No other book goes into so much detail about Justin's dating dreams or tells all the secrets from the My World Tour.

Read all about Justin's favourite girls, the advice Usher gave Justin and why he isn't your average teenage boy. Find out what pranks Justin likes to pull and what it was like to go behind the scenes at The White House!

Sarah Oliver is a celebrity journalist and biographer. In Justin Bieber A–Z she opens the door to Justin Bieber's world and invites you in.

You can follow Sarah on Twitter (http:// Twitter.com/SarahOliverAtoZ).

You can read this book from start to finish, or dip in and out of it, as you prefer.

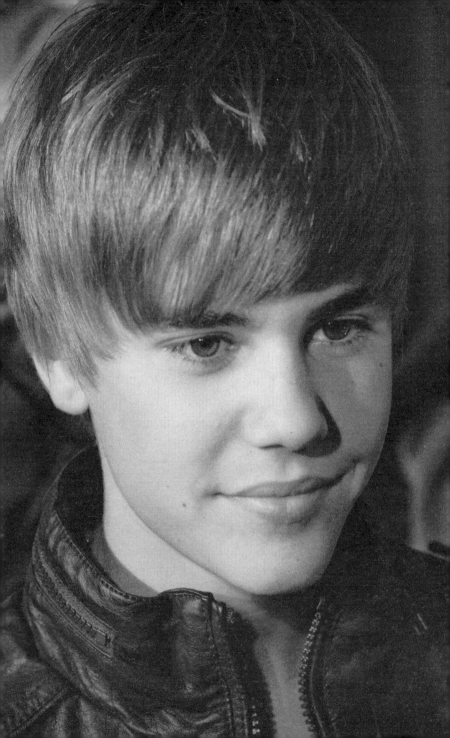

A is for...

Accidents

Justin may only be in his teens but he's had his fair share of accidents on stage and off stage.

When Justin was seven he was locked in a toy box by his cousin whilst playing hide-and-seek. Poor Justin was having fun but when he found he couldn't get out he started to panic. He has hated being in cramped places ever since. A few years later when he was 11 he had another traumatic experience when the lift he was travelling in got stuck. He was trapped in there for four hours as specialist lift engineers had to be called and they were two hours away. It was a truly awful day for Justin and he must have been so glad when it was over. He admits now that he's claustrophobic and hates it when he has to go in lifts with lots of other people – he's scared it's going to happen again.

Justin told Maclean's magazine: "I'm a really claustrophobic person to begin with. I hate elevators, especially crammed elevators. I get really scared. So I think that it's very definitely scary when girls are all around me and I can't go anywhere. At the same time, I guess I got to get used to it, you know what I mean?"

Whilst performing he has hurt himself a few times. He fell on stage when he was performing 'Love Me' at the Q102 Jingle Ball in December 2010. He jumped straight back up and carried on, even though it looked like he had hurt his leg. Fans in the audience couldn't work out whether he had done it on purpose because he reacted so well. That just shows how professional Justin is. He won't let anything ruin things for his fans.

Only a month earlier he had injured his knee during a performance in Cleveland. He tweeted afterwards: "Busted my knee last night in the middle of the show. Not fun. Finished the show with a sweet limp.

"Knee is swollen today but all good, Spending quality time with @studiomama."

Studiomama is his mum Pattie's twitter name.

The biggest accident that Justin has had so far was when he was supporting Taylor Swift during her Fearless concert at Wembley. Justin explained what happened to journalist Nicholas Kohler from Macleans.ca. He said: "My foot broke at the beginning of the song – I was running and there was a little dip in the stage and I rolled my ankle real bad and broke it – so it was definitely a struggle to finish the song. But I really didn't want to let my fans down and they were looking for a show so I had to give it to them." Justin was rushed to hospital as soon as he came off stage so he wasn't around for the encore. The doctors told him he had broken his foot but instead of having a normal plaster cast put on his leg he made sure they gave him an Aircast leg brace so he could still perform. He couldn't have coped if he had been banned from performing for several weeks. The special leg brace had air cushions inside that held Justin's leg and foot in the right position so it could heal, and a hard outer shell to protect it from knocks. Justin looked so cute with his cast on.

Only hours after having his leg brace fitted Justin was back on stage supporting Taylor in Manchester. Later that week he released a fun video with Taylor where he talked about the accident.

Justin said: "You told me, 'Break a leg'... I couldn't break a leg but I broke a foot for you."

JUSTIN WAS SUPPORTING HIS FRIEND TAYLOR SWIFT AT WEMBLEY WHEN HE BROKE HIS FOOT.

Taylor smiled and explained to Justin: "It's kind of like a figurative statement. I was like, 'Good luck! It's so good to have you! Break a leg!'…"

Justin cheekily interrupted: "I just wanted to do what you told me. I'm so sorry."

Taylor added: "I wish I had clarified that."

Smiling Justin said: "I guess tonight I'm going to have to perform sitting down."

Turning to the camera, Taylor spoke directly to all of Justin's fans watching at home: "All joking aside, he broke his foot on stage in front of 11,000 people and finished the song!"

Justin now says breaking his foot onstage was his most embarrassing moment ever. It will take something big to top it.

Sometimes accidents happen that don't directly involve Justin but can impact on him and what he is doing. On Saturday 4th December 2010 he was supposed to be appearing on a German TV variety show called *Wetten, Dass..?* but it was cancelled after one of the performers on before Justin seriously injured himself doing a stunt which involved doing somersaults over five cars on stilts. Justin asked his fans to pray for the injured performer. He tweeted: "Just want to let my people in Germany know I won't be on Wetten Dass tonight as an accident has taken place and … we all don't think it is right to continue. Please pray for Samuel Koch & his family as we wait and hope for his health and safety.

"Germany I'm sorry we couldn't perform tonight but some things are more important than putting on a show. We will be back I promise. Thank u"

Justin's fans started to pray and #prayforsamuel soon started trending on Twitter.

On other occasions Justin's fans have been injured waiting to see him. Eight fans were rushed to hospital after they were crushed at Sydney's Circular Quay. They had been hoping to see Justin perform in a free show but so many people turned up that things got out of hand. The Australian police ended up cancelling the show because so many young fans turned up without parents.

The show released a statement shortly afterwards saying: "Global phenomenon Justin Bieber's only Australian public performance caused such an enormous crowd to descend on Sydney's Overseas Passenger Terminal that police had to cancel it due to safety concerns.

"As of 4.30am, Monday 26 April, the police shut the gates to the area and said that due to safety concerns no more fans would be permitted into the area. Around 5.20am, with the forecourt area at full capacity and fans still arriving, the police ordered Sunrise to cancel the performance."

Justin wanted to apologise to the fans and tweeted afterwards: "With everything that happened 2day i want u all 2 know that i care and U all rule and if i could thank every 1 of u individually i would.

"I love my fans....and I am just as disappointed as everyone else with the news from this morning. I want to sing for my fans."

Acting

Justin might be most famous for his singing but he is a talented actor as well. He just needs more opportunities to show off his talent.

On 23 September 2010 he appeared in an episode of American crime series CSI. He played the part of Jason McCann, a teenager with a bad streak in the season premiere. It was a big deal for Justin and he loved being on the set and wearing an orange jumpsuit. He tweeted a picture of a man leading him away with the caption: "...and I told you I was a BAD MAN!!" He also got someone to take a photo of him standing next to a fake corpse holding a dismembered arm.

Carol Mendelsohn, the CSI executive producer, told MTV: "I thought that he did a really good job. We only had Justin for a day, for ten-and-a-half hours, and he had a lot of work crammed into those 10 and a half hours."

Justin did so well that he was asked whether he would like to be in another episode in February 2011. Justin jumped at the chance!

Justin would like to act in films as well as in TV dramas. He would be interested in doing a remake of *Grease* one day and told a reporter from *The Sun* that he would pick Miley Cyrus to play Sandy and Susan Boyle to play Principal McGee. If he was in charge he'd make sure there were more famous faces in the cast too.

He really rates Susan Boyle and said: "Wouldn't Susan Boyle make an amazing Principal McGee? We'd just need to write it into the script that she broke into song. I am obsessed with Susan. When I look at her original audition it makes the hairs on the back of my neck stand up."

Albums

Justin used to dream that he would have his own album one day so when it actually happened he was blown away. He was so excited about seeing his own album available in the shops next to albums by John Mayer and *American Idol* winner Kris Allen. Justin's first album was called *My World* and it was released on 17 November 2009 in Canada and the USA, 20 November 2009 in Australia

Justin is a massive Susan Boyle fan.

and 18 January 2010 in the UK. It contained seven tracks plus two bonus tracks (the second bonus track was only available on the Canadian version of the album).

Normally the first album an artist releases shares the artist's name but Justin was allowed to pick his own title for the album. He came up with the idea of calling it *My World* because he had recorded a song called 'My World' (but the track didn't end up making the album). Justin thought that 'My World' summed up the album because all the tracks talked about things that were in his world: love, girls, his parents splitting up, family, school. His manager Scooter, mentor Usher and the people from his record company loved the name.

Track listing for *My World*
1. One Time
2. Favourite Girl
3. Down to Earth
4. Bigger
5. One Less Lonely Girl
6. First Dance (featuring Usher)
7. Love Me

Bonus tracks
8. Common Denominator
9. One Less Lonely Girl

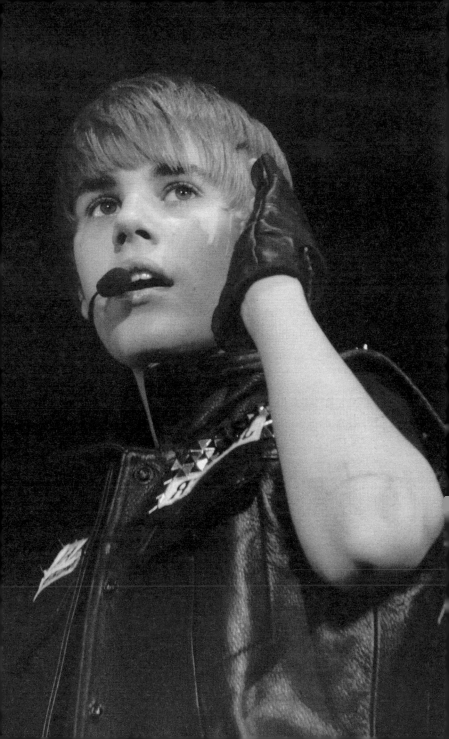

The second part of the album was called *My World 2.0* and fans had to wait until 19 March 2010 to get their hands on it. It had originally been scheduled to come out during Valentines week in February so it was a month later than planned. It showed a different side to Justin as he explained to chron.com: "I wanted to do something that was a little bit more R&B and that could reach out to everyone. I just wanted to be able to show my vocal abilities. 'Up' is one of my favourites on the album. I like everything about it."

Justin was glad that the album came out in two parts because it meant that fans didn't have to wait over a year like they normally do with other artists' albums.

Track listing for *My World 2.0*
1. Baby
2. Somebody to Love
3. Stuck in the Moment
4. U Smile
5. Runaway Love
6. Never Let You Go
7. Overboard (featuring Jessica Jarrell)
8. Eenie Meenie (with Sean Kingston)
9. Up
10. That should Be Me

Bonus tracks
11. Kiss and Tell (Japan and iTunes)
12. Where Are You Now (Japan, Australia and
    Walmart copies)

In November 2010 Justin released a third album
called *My Worlds Acoustic*. He confessed why he decided
to release an acoustic album to MTV: "I really think
that I did an acoustic album because there's a lot of
haters out there that say, 'Justin Bieber can't sing. His
voice is all Auto-Tuned.'

"I think kind of stripping it down and having it kind
of really mellow and being able to hear my voice is why
I wanted to do it."

USA fans could only buy the album from Walmart
stores but fans from other countries could buy an album
called *My Worlds: The Collection* which was the acoustic
album plus some tracks from his first two albums. The
international album had a total of 31 songs on the two-
disc set.

Justin was so clever to release an acoustic album
because after listening to it no one would be able to say
he couldn't sing. Fans love listening to all the tracks on
the album, especially 'Baby' and the new track 'Pray'.

Track listing for *My Worlds Acoustic*
1. One Time
2. Baby
3. One Less Lonely Girl
4. Down to Earth
5. U Smile
6. Stuck in the Moment
7. Favourite Girl (live)
8. That Should Be Me
9. Never Say Never (Featuring Jaden Smith)
10. Pray

When Justin released an official video for 'Pray' he sent a special message to his fans. In it he said: "I wrote this song thinking of Michael Jackson's Man in the Mirror and we are donating a portion of the proceeds from every album sold to Children's Miracle Network Hospitals. This song means a lot to me and I love this video. I hope you all do too and please support the *My Worlds Acoustic* album at Walmart now. Thanks so much. I love music and I love your support of my dream. We will never stop. This is just the beginning. Chase your dreams and always try to make a positive difference in others' lives."

Justin says he wanted to give something back to his

fans and God. He wanted to make a difference and felt like the Children's Miracle Network was a worthy cause. He had met people from the charity for the first time back in September 2009 when he performed in New York and knew they would use the money raised wisely.

The President of Children's Miracle Network, Scott Burt, told the *International Business Times*: "Justin's generous contributions from his new album will make a meaningful difference in saving lives of the children treated at our children's hospitals. As an organization that donates the most money of any charity to children's hospitals around the country, we are extremely grateful for his support. With the proceeds, we will be able to create even more miracles for children."

When Billboard announced the Top Ten Biggest Selling Albums of 2010 in the USA Justin's fans were thrilled to see him on the list. They thought he fully deserved to be there because his albums had been so good.

BILLBOARD'S TOP TEN ALBUMS:

1. *Recovery* by Eminem – 3,415,000 copies sold
2. *Need You Now* by Lady Antebellum – 3,089,000 copies sold

3. *Speak Now* by Taylor Swift – 2,960,000 copies sold

4. *My World 2.0* by Justin Bieber – 2,319,000 copies sold

5 *The Gift* by Susan Boyle – 1,852,000 copies sold

6. *The Fame* by Lady Gaga – 1,591,000 copies sold

7. *Soldier of Love* by Sade – 1,300,000 copies sold

8. *Thank Me Later* by Drake – 1,269,000 copies sold

9. *Raymond V Raymond* by Usher – 1,183,000 copies sold

10. *Animal* by Ke$ha– 1,143,000 copies sold

Justin was asked by Macleans.ca why his CD was such a success. He replied: "I got to work with a lot of great producers and a lot of great writers. I got to work with (Christopher) 'Tricky' (Stewart) and The-Dream, who wrote 'Obsessed' by Mariah Carey. The album was just a blast and I think that having so much fun was reflected in the album. I think people saw that."

JUSTIN POSES WITH HIS
TROPHIES AT THE
AMERICAN MUSIC
AWARDS 2010.

Awards

You don't get to be as talented a musician as Justin without winning an award or two. Justin has done exceptionally well over the last two years, and in a few year's time he might end up with enough trophies to fill a whole room full of trophy cabinets!

In 2010 he won four American Music Awards (Artist of the Year, Favourite Pop/Rock Male Artist, T-Mobile Breakthrough Artist, Favourite Pop/Rock Album). He picked up two awards in Brazil: a Meus Prêmios Nick Award for Favourite International Artist and an MTV Brazil Music Award for International Artist. He was nominated for four other MTV awards and managed to walk away with three of them – Best Male and Best Push Act at the Europe Awards and Best New Artist at the Video Awards. He just missed out on Best New Act at the Europe Awards as Ke$ha was given the award.

Justin won three awards at the Much Music Awards: Favourite Canadian Video, New Artist Award and Best International Video By A Canadian for 'Baby'. He was also nominated for Best International Video By A Canadian for 'One Time'.

He also picked up a Myx Music Award for Favourite International Video, four Teen Choice Awards, one TRL Award and one Young Hollywood Award.

In total Justin was nominated for 28 awards in 2010

and won 19 of them. 2011 looks set to be an even bigger year for Justin. He was over the moon when he was nominated for two Grammys in 2011 – it was an amazing achievement to get nominated so early in his career.

Justin was nominated for Best New Artist and Best Pop Vocal Album (for *My World 2.0*). He had been so excited to attend the Grammys in 2010 that the thought of being nominated must have rocked his world. He had tweeted back in January 2010: "Super stoked. its crazy. last year i was watching the grammys now i get to be there. get to meet some of my heroes. Insane"

Selena Gomez really wanted him to win the Best New Artist Grammy in 2011. MTV asked her who she wanted to win and she said: "I would have to say Bieber just because I know how hard he works, I hope he wins, but I love Drake as well. It's a really hard category so I don't know who's going to win, but of course I have to say Bieber."

Justin was up against Drake, Florence and the Machine, Mumford & Sons and Esperanza Spalding in the Best New Artist category. In the Best Pop Vocal Album category his *My World 2.0* album was up against *I Dreamed a Dream* by Susan Boyle, *The Fame Monster* by Lady Gaga, *Battle Studies* by John Mayer and *Teenage Dream* by Katy Perry.

At first Justin thought he had been nominated for just one Grammy but then his manager Scooter rang him to say he'd been nominated for another one. Justin explained what happened to his fans via Twitter:

"just went to bed and thought i was nominated for 1 #grammy and was already freakin out…then @scooterbraun just called me…2 NOMINATIONS!!"

"win or lose…this is #CRAZY!! the GRAMMYS!!! #HOLYCRAP!!! WOOOHOOO …ok ok..need to sleep. ARE U KIDDING ME!! #HOLYCRAP!!"

As well as winning a lot of awards over the last two years from award shows Justin has also received awards from his record company when his singles and albums have sold thousands of copies. He received a Golden Disc back in November when he was in Madrid in Spain for *My Worlds: The Collection*. His first album *My World* went Platinum three months after it was released which meant that Justin had sold a million copies. It went double platinum in December 2010 – two million copies had been sold by that point. The second part of the album also went double platinum – Justin was so thankful to all his fans who had gone out and bought a copy.

It's not just Justin who is ecstatic when he wins an award. His parents, Scooter, Usher and everyone connected to him want him to do well and when he wins an award they are so happy for him. They showed how much they loved him when they surprised him with a big cake after he won his four American Music Awards. He was performing in Toronto in Canada and all his friends and family came on stage clapping and cheering. Justin looked surprised but happy at the same time, it's not every day that you're presented with a cake with candles on, when it's not even your birthday.

When Justin won his American Music Awards it was especially moving for his mentor Usher because Justin had beaten him in the Pop/Rock Favourite Male Artist category and won the biggest award of the night, Favorite Artist of the Year. Usher hadn't even been in the running for that award so Justin had beaten him just by being nominated in the first place. Usher ended up crying with happiness as he explained to the cameras backstage: "To see Justin take the award – having received that award before – it was like an out-of-body experience, you understand?

"It was emotional. I don't cry that often, but I did. Hopefully it gives an indication of how hard we worked to build a career that hopefully will flourish and blossom over the years."

In his acceptance speech Justin said: "Wow... this means... I don't know what else to say... my fans are amazing. I want to thank my label. I want to thank L.A. Reid, Steve Bartels, Chris Hicks. I wanna thank everybody, my mom for giving up so much for me, my family, my dad... but you know, I really got this opportunity, really about a year and a half ago, I really was embraced by a man named Usher Raymond and I don't know but I feel like he's had such an amazing career and it would only be right if I invited him up here to share it with me. Not only my mentor but my best friend, my big brother, I love you man."

Usher gave him a huge hug when he got on stage and they walked off with their arms around each other. They are going to be friends forever.

Justin hasn't just won awards for his music. In October 2010 he picked up the Hottest Hottie Award at the Australian Nickelodeon Kids' Choice Awards. He had been up against Taylor Lautner, Taylor Swift and Rachael Finch. He is going to win a lot more awards for being gorgeous as he grows up.

USHER WAS INCREDIBLY PROUD OF HIS PROTÉGÉ AFTER JUSTIN WON FAVORITE ARTIST OF THE YEAR AT THE AMERICAN MUSIC AWARDS.

JUSTIN BEAT THE LIKES OF *TWILIGHT* STAR TAYLOR LAUTNER TO THE HOTTEST HOTTIE AWARD AT THE AUSTRALIAN NICKELODEON KIDS' CHOICE AWARDS.

B is for...

Best Friends

Justin's best friends in the whole world are Ryan Butler and Chaz Somers. They have been the best of friends since they started playing hockey together when they were about seven or eight. They went to Stratford Central Secondary School together and caused all kinds of mischief but they weren't bad boys – they just liked having fun. Ryan and Chaz were gutted when Justin had to leave school to move to Atlanta but they were happy for him at the same time.

Justin told MTV: "I went to school until I was 13 and

my best friends (Chaz and Ryan) are still there. I miss them, but this is definitely worth it.

"I get to fly them over to see me pretty regularly."

When Justin was at school he had been really good at sport and some kids in his class had picked on him and tried to say that he was a show-off but he wasn't. He was just naturally gifted. Having Chaz and Ryan to talk to must have really helped Justin because they could always make him smile. Most people only have one best friend but Justin was blessed with two best friends.

Since moving away Justin has stayed in really close contact with Chaz and Ryan. They talk on the phone all the time and they can go and visit any time they want. Whenever there is a big event or something that Justin thinks the others would be interested in he lets them know and arranges the flights.

Justin has taken his best friends with him to meet celebrities. He enjoyed having his photo taken with Ryan and Eminem when they were in Detroit. He tweeted "Detroit was nuts…had to pay respect to that guy from 8 mile. EMINEM is a beast." Justin actually performed Eminem's 'Lose Yourself' on stage that night.

Justin told *Bliss* magazine: "Yeah, my two best friends come along with me sometimes. One of them, Ryan, you've probably seen in my video ('One Time'). They're proud of me, so it's nice to share cool stuff like that with them."

As well as appearing in the video for 'One Time', Ryan also appeared in the video for 'Somebody to Love'. In the second video Ryan stands next to Justin wearing a t-shirt advertising his twitter account. If you blink you might miss it though, so if you want to see it go to YouTube and it's at 2 mins 50 seconds. Since he appeared on the video Ryan has gained more followers and he now has over 230,000. Head over to http:// twitter.com/itsryanbutler to learn more about Ryan and what he gets up to with Justin.

Ryan's highlight of 2010 was going on tour with Justin and in the future he would love to be a big Hollywood director or editor. Chaz is also on twitter but he only has 24,000 followers – but that is still a lot for a regular guy from Canada. He is considering deleting his twitter account so follow him while you can http://twitter.com/chazilla94.

Justin thanked Ryan and Chaz for helping him "stay just Justin" in his album sleeve. Journalist Nicholas Kohler from Macleans.ca asked Justin how they do it. He said: "They're very happy for me but they really don't care about any of this. They like me for me. When we're hanging out and I say something stupid or something, they're not going to treat me like I'm a superstar, by any

JUSTIN IS A MASSIVE FAN OF EMINEM AND HAS COVERED ONE OF THE RAPPER'S SONGS DURING HIS OWN LIVE PERFORMANCES.

means. They're not going to treat me like I'm bigger than everybody else. They're just going to treat me like Justin. They're going to pop me in the head and not care. I get to see them at least once a month. I get to fly them out to wherever I am. I've flown them out to L.A. and Atlanta. I think it's really important to just have your close friends around you. We're very active, we play basketball and hockey and soccer and stuff. We go to the movies with girls and stuff like regular teenage boys."

Ryan's family have to deal with a son who is famous for being Justin Bieber's best friend. Girls from all over the world somehow get the Butler's home phone number and ring him for a chat. At Christmas his mum unplugged the phone for a few days so they could have some peace and quiet. Family friends and even teachers at Ryan's school have asked if he can get them tickets to one of Justin's concerts. Many see Ryan as the nearest thing to Justin so try and get him to contact Justin for them. Ryan, Chaz and most residents in Stratford have been asked at some point where Justin's old apartment is or where his grandparents live by fans who are visiting the town. They don't tell them though because they think Justin's family deserve some privacy. They would hate it if the whole family moved out of the area because that might stop Justin coming back as often.

Another of Justin's close friends is Dan Kanter. Dan

is Justin's lead guitarist and musical director. He is also a songwriter and producer and comes from Toronto in Canada. If you want to follow him on Twitter, his address is http://twitter.com/DANKANTER. Justin loves performing with Dan and jumped at the chance to perform at his wedding in October 2010. Justin, Dan and the other musicians performed 'Get Down Tonight' by KC and the Sunshine band and the traditional Jewish song 'Hava Nagila'. Dan and his bride couldn't have a long honeymoon because Dan had to be in Hawaii with Justin soon after the wedding.

Justin likes to call his best friends his wolf pack. As well as Dan there are dancers Antonio and Marvin and a few others like rapper Asher Roth. Justin knows they are always up for a laugh and will be there for him, no matter what. Justin met Asher Roth when he first moved to Atlanta. Asher sees Justin as a little brother and remembers fondly how he used to play Rock Band at his house. They met because Scooter was also Asher's talent manager and he introduced them.

Birthdays

Justin was born on the 1st March 1994 in the Canadian city of London, but grew up in a small town called Stratford.

With each new birthday Justin can reflect on everything he has achieved in the year leading up to this date. Most people just go from one birthday to the next without achieving much but for each year since he was 12 Justin has done something extra special:

- When he was **12** he entered a local talent competition and his mum posted videos on YouTube. Talent manager Scooter Braun saw them and convinced Justin he was the manager for him.
- When he was **13** the video of him singing Chris Brown's 'With You' had one million hits on YouTube.
- When he was **14** he chose Usher as his mentor, over Justin Timberlake.
- When he was **15** he released his first single.
- When he was **16** he did his first tour of the USA and Canada.

Justin's 16th birthday was one he will never forget. He was surrounded by his closet friends and family – and he was given some amazing gifts. He revealed all on the *Live From Studio Five* TV show. Justin said: "I was in L.A. (for my birthday). I went to L.A. first and I had a party out there for all my friends and stuff and then we went to Toronto and did a family party up there.

(Usher) helped buy me a car. He bought me a Range Rover. Yeah I can drive." Host Ian Wright was a bit cheeky and when Justin admitted that he failed his driving test the first time Ian hinted that he couldn't reach the pedals. Justin didn't get offended though. He is used to people making comments about his height.

Justin had been promised another car for his birthday by P. Diddy. Justin told MTV: "He said when I turn 16 he was going to give me his Lamborghini. But we all know Diddy's not gonna give me his Lamborghini. He's all talk." It's thought that Justin spoke too soon because he was snapped by the paparazzi driving the Lamborghini so maybe P. Diddy did hand over the keys to his car after all.

Justin's first birthday party was for his friends from L.A. and the music business. It was a house party but it wasn't held in his own house – probably in case it got trashed. They rented a villa and everyone Justin wanted to be there was sent a very special invitation. It was the best party – there was sumo wrestling, swimming, basketball, karaoke, paintball, laser tag... and delicious food. The villa was in a private area so no paparazzi were able to get close. The only photos that were taken were the ones Justin and his mates took. If you Google 'Justin Bieber 16th party photos' you will be able to see a cute picture of Justin as a sumo

JUSTIN CHOSE USHER AS HIS MENTOR OVER FELLOW MUSICIAN–TURNED–
ACTOR, JUSTIN TIMBERLAKE (*ABOVE*).

wrestler, Usher and Justin smiling, the cinema room all decorated with balloons and some of Justin's friends playing in the pool.

After the party finished and everyone had left the villa Justin headed to the airport and flew home to Canada. His second party was held at a bowling alley in Toronto.

Justin tweeted: "Gonna go birthday bowling 2night with family and friends ... not gonna dance in the lanes though.

"Thanks to everyone for the birthday wishes. u guys all changed my life and are giving me a great birthday. appreciate it. 'Baby' and 'Never Let You Go' are both top 10 and rising!!! Wow!! U r all the greatest fans in the world!!! Great birthday gift. Thank u."

Justin also spent some of his birthday weekend in the company of basketball player Kobe Bryant who plays for the Los Angeles Lakers. Justin loved watching the Lakers win and saw Canada win 2-0 in the final of the women's hockey at the Winter Olympics. He couldn't see the match live but he watched it on TV while he was watching the Lakers live.

Books

Justin used to love the storybook *We're Going on a Bear Hunt* when he was growing up. He loved hearing about the family who go on a journey to find a bear. Justin isn't unique in loving this classic storybook written by Michael Rosen and illustrated by Helen Oxenbury. It has been a bedtime favourite for thousands of children since it first came out 20 years ago.

His favourite book at the moment is *Fledgling: Jason Steed* by Mark A. Cooper. Jaden Smith recommended it to him, and Justin is so glad he did. Jaden and Justin recorded 'Never Say Never' for the movie The Karate Kid together. Jaden played the main character Dre Parker in the movie about a young boy who is taught karate by an old karate master. He is also Will Smith's son and Justin meets up with him whenever he has some free time and they hang out together.

Justin enjoyed reading about Jason, a young boy who wants to be in the SAS when he grows up and ends up getting involved in a military operation whilst on a summer camp with the sea cadets. Justin even found himself crying during some touching parts. It was the first book in a series so Justin will no doubt be reading *Revenge of Boudica: Jason Steed* when it comes out later this year.

NBA Basketball player Kobe Bryant plays for Justin's favourite team, L.A. Lakers.

Another book that Justin loves is *Percy Jackson and the Olympians: The Lighting Thief* by Rick Riordan. He thinks it's a great book and would recommend that his fans check it out. He also thinks people of any age should pick up a Bible and read it. Justin told Scholastic: "There are many lessons in *The Bible* that you can apply to your everyday life."

Last year Justin wrote his own book *First Step 2 Forever: My Story*. It was a big hit in America, Canada and all around the world. He did book signings in many cities and lots of fans left on cloud nine after meeting him and getting a hug. Justin tweeted in November 2010: "wow. FIRST STEP 2 FOREVER is on the NY TIMES BESTSELLER List again. 5 weeks straight!! Thank u all so much. Hope u all r enjoying the book."

Bullying

Justin has gone through life being bullied by people who are jealous of his talent. When he was at school they enjoyed picking on him because he was good at sport and was small for his age. Justin wouldn't let the bullies say anything bad about his family though and he would hit back if they did. Justin would never ever bully someone but he wasn't a walkover.

Justin wanted to try and help victims of bullying

when he became famous and so he joined the 'It Gets Better Project'. It's an anti-bullying campaign and Justin helped by recording a special video message. In the video Justin talks about how victims need to speak out and tell someone, and that bullying isn't cool. Justin added: "If you're a bystander, make sure to step in and, you know, help out." It's good that Justin asked people who witness someone getting bullied to do something because these others are not normally part of anti-bullying campaigns. Usually the bully and the victim are the sole focus of attention.

Justin still gets bullied every day by gossip site journalists, bloggers and people in forums. They love writing things they know will upset Justin and his fans. Justin discussed the bullies who write hurtful things on his YouTube pages with American chat show host Ellen DeGeneres. He said: "There are so many bullies, it goes on so much... everybody goes through bullying... even me. On my YouTube page there are so many haters. They just say crazy stuff."

Busking

Justin started busking outside the Avon Theatre in his hometown when he was 12 to make money and to perform. He came up with the idea because he wanted to go golfing with his friends but he didn't have the money he needed. He had not long before competed in The Stratford Star talent competition and it had made him want to perform more.

He thought that if he sat down on the steps of the Avon Theatre with his guitar he might be able to impress people with his singing voice and they might chuck some money into his guitar case. He made nearly $200 the first day and decided that he would save up the money so that he could go to Disney World at the end of the summer with his mum.

The Avon Theatre on George Street East was the perfect location because it was a busy theatre, with lots of tourists who would wait outside before the show started. He had a captive audience because in the summer the town's Shakespeare Festival was on and hundreds of people were milling around the area where he positioned himself.

Some people were so impressed with Justin that they recorded him and put the videos on YouTube. He performed a real mix of songs so there was something for everyone. He sang Christian songs, pop songs and classic tracks too. He told *Rolling Stone* magazine: "I sang 'I'll Be' by Edwin McCain, 'You and Me' by Lifehouse, 'U Got It Bad' by Usher and 'Cry Me A River' by Justin Timberlake." Another

JUSTIN OPENED HIS HEART TO CHAT SHOW HOST ELLEN DEGENERES.

favourite from his busking days was 'Refine Me' by Jennifer Knapp.

The people who saw him busk also checked out the videos his mum had put up on YouTube from the talent competition. They told their friends about Justin and started leaving lovely messages about him and his talent. For the first time Justin started to have fans.

Thankfully some schoolgirls on a trip filmed Justin as he sang away and decided to post the footage they took on YouTube. Their video is the only one of Justin busking that fans can see, as his mum didn't video him and post it up like she did for his talent show performances.

Since Justin has made the big time the house manager of The Avon Theatre has spoken to his local paper the *Star* about how nice Justin was when he used to busk outside. Eldon Gammon remembers Justin as the "Little guy with the big voice." He told the reporter: "It almost seemed like the guitar was bigger than him. Student groups, they poured around him. The five-minute call would go – it's an announcement that you could hear all over – and then we would have to drag them away from him. He had a good persona with people. He was always very polite, always said 'Thank you'. It's interesting that the music he's doing now is nothing like what he did here."

DID YOU KNOW?

When Justin was visiting the UK he decided to go to Buckingham Palace with his guitarist Dan and do a bit of busking. They did a medley of some of Justin's best tracks and amazed passers-by who stopped to watch. Around 30 people enjoyed watching Justin perform and the pair posed for photos afterwards. Justin loved it but they didn't make any money, as they didn't put down any guitar cases for people to drop money into. Justin loved having the opportunity to busk again.

C is for...

Caitlin

Caitlin is a very close friend of Justin's who was in a very serious boating accident whilst Justin was performing in Germany. Justin's friends had texted and left messages on his phone to tell him what had happened and that she might not pull through but Justin didn't get them until he returned home. He was absolutely devastated and called Caitlin's family as soon as he could.

Justin talked to *Twist* magazine about what happened. He said: "I was scared, so I immediately called up Caitlin's family, and they weren't picking up the phone, so I got really nervous. I kept calling and texting and finally I got in contact with Caitlin's mom. I talked to her on the phone for about 20 minutes and she was crying. It was tough. Caitlin's actually my ex-girlfriend, I dated her about six months ago, so it was hard because she's still a good friend.

"I went to the hospital to visit and she looked really bad. She had all of these IVs in her, and she couldn't speak at all. I brought her a Build-a-Bear because we had always wanted to make one together and we never got a chance to do it. So, I went and built her a bear and brought it to her in the hospital. I dressed it up as me, I even put a little baseball cap on it. Caitlin was very lucky that she survived, and now she's doing a lot better. She's in physical therapy where she's learning how to walk again, so that's good."

It is a miracle that Caitlin survived because her injuries were so severe. She actually died on her way to the hospital but was revived. Justin's fans were so sorry to hear what had happened and instantly started praying for Caitlin.

Canada

Justin is a proud Canadian and he wants the world to know it!

He loves everything Canadian, from hockey to maple syrup – and he always supports fellow Canadian performers. He might tour all around the world but Canada will always be home and he tries to visit as often as he can.

Because Justin comes from Canada he is used to coping with snow as they get quite a lot of snow in his hometown of Stratford. He found it strange how the UK fell to pieces when a few inches of snow fell. He told Digital Spy: "You guys are acting like it's the end of the world – everything's cancelled and the subway's not working – but in Canada this is, like, the least amount of snow we get. We have to have at least 10 feet of snow to get a day off school."

He also had some advice for people caught up in the snow: "You guys aren't wearing the right sort of clothes. You need to wear hats, scarves, mitts… and long johns! I always wear long johns when it's cold. I know they're not cool but I'd rather be warm than cold."

Celebrity Fans

Justin has so many celebrity fans. They love his personality, his cuteness and his music.

One of his biggest celebrity fans is Rihanna. She kissed Justin back in December 2009 when he presented

RIHANNA, ONE OF JUSTIN'S MANY CELEBRITY FANS.

her with some flowers at a launch party. It was only on the cheek but Justin told reporters he wasn't going to wash his face. Since then they have hung out a few times.

In November 2010 she tweeted: "Justin Bieber just flashed me his abs in the middle of a restaurant! Wow! He actually had a lil 6 pack! Sexy, lol! #Beliebersplzdontkillme."

Some people have suggested that the two of them would make a cute couple but it doesn't look like it's going to happen. Justin admitted to talk show host Chelsea Handler: "Yeah, I asked her out. It didn't go so well since I'm not with her. I asked her out and she was basically like, 'You're too young.'"

Justin's first ever celebrity fan wasn't Usher as many people think, but Ne-Yo. He saw a video of Justin performing one of his songs when he was only 11. Ne-Yo told *The Sun*: "Justin did a cover of one of my songs on YouTube which created a buzz.

"He came to a show and performed and was incredible then. But I didn't do anything because he was 11.

"I have no regrets. Things happen for a reason. He wasn't supposed to be signed to me. Usher has done good. Where he is now is where he's meant to be."

Ne-Yo might not have stepped in and got Justin a

NE-YO WAS JUSTIN'S FIRST CELEBRITY FAN.

record deal when he was 11 but Justin still thinks he's great. He posted on his Facebook wall: "I got discovered singing your song SO SICK. thanks for the love. Big fan of Ne-Yo. Dude is a Beast."

Justin has quite a few British celebrity fans, including the whole of the Beckham family. They have been to watch him in concert and they chat to him at Lakers games. The Lakers are the Los Angeles basketball team. Russell Brand and his wife Katy Perry think he is really cute and Brand told a reporter from *E!*: "We want our own Justin Bieber. We can't have the actual one because he's busy with his work."

The *Glee* cast want to kidnap him for an episode too. Lea Michele, who plays Rachel Berry, thinks Justin would be an awesome addition to the Glee cast and one of the show's creators, Ryan Murphy, has said he would write him in if he wanted to appear in an episode. They have already included one of his songs in an episode but Justin's fans want more.

People say that imitation is the sincerest form of flattery and Justin has had quite a few celebrities pretend to be him in the last year. When Michael Bublé needed to promote his single 'Hollywood' he could have picked any celebrity in the world to imitate but he picked Justin. In the video he wore a purple t-shirt and turquoise hoodie, and said his name was

Michael Bieber. He danced around and shook his hair like Justin does.

Michael told *PopEater*: "My last video and single 'Haven't Met You' was about everyone's dream of finding a relationship and love. This time around, it's about celebrity culture and people's dreams about fame and what can go along with that. It's about having fun but remembering where you came from and what's real. You can see how much fun I had playing all those characters."

Actress and comedienne Kathy Griffin decided to film her own trailer for Justin's movie *Never Say Never* in which she played the main part. She mocked Justin as she pretended to lose her voice, rejected a young fan and wrote Baby, Baby, Baby on a note pad. Some people might have found it funny when it aired on *Jimmy Kimmel Live* but Justin's fans didn't.

Charity Work

Justin strongly believes that God wants him to use his wealth for good and he helps as many charities as he can. His favourite charity is Pencils of Promise which was set up by Adam Braun. He explains on their official website: "Pencils of Promise is now a global movement of passionate individuals committed to supporting a world

KATY PERRY AND RUSSELL BRAND ARE BIG JUSTIN BIEBER FANS.

with greater educational opportunity for all. Thousands have joined us, making contributions through acts both large and small.

"Our role is to create more than just four walls; the schools we build must continue to provide generations of quality education. To succeed, our approach works from the bottom up, finding and working with communities who don't just need a school, but who are investing in creating a successful one."

Justin made sure that he gave back to the community during his tour of the USA and Canada. For every ticket purchased Justin gave one dollar to Pencils of Promise.

Justin doesn't just send the money to Adam, he has been and got his hands dirty too. His charity work even earned him an award at the *World Leadership Awards 2010* in August. Instead of taking all the credit himself Justin called Adam on stage to tell people more about the charity. He wants to spread the word so they can build as many schools as possible.

Pencils of Promise might be Justin's main charity but he also helps other charities around the world.

He decided to raise some money for the Great Ormond Street Hospital Charity which helps sick children and their families by setting up a special eBay auction. Justin donated lots of his clothes and sneakers and fans bid as much as they possibly could to try and secure something Justin had worn in the past. He actually visited the hospital and spent time with the children there too – something that not many pop stars would do. The top prize in the auction was tickets to one of his concerts and the winner would get to meet Justin too. The winning bidder paid £3,433.33 and Justin didn't take a penny of it, it all went to charity.

Justin also helps charities in other ways, even if he isn't personally involved. When 'Gravity' singer John Mayer recorded a special message on raising awareness of the disease malaria he used Justin to get through to people how deadly the disease is. He said: "Almost a million people every year die from malaria, and of that number, 85 per cent die under the age of Justin Bieber. With your help, by buying a malaria net for just 10 dollars, we can help, by the end of the year, to get these kids to Bieber. Next year we'll go Jonas Brothers; after that Twilight kids, but baby steps, baby steps. Let's get them to Bieber."

Justin is a great role model for young people as he is proof that you don't have to be an adult to help people. He has encouraged his fans to help charities like Pencils of Promise and other charities special to them. He strongly believes that everyone can make a difference. In October 2010 he went along to Variety's 4th *Annual Power Of Youth Event* held at Paramount Studios in Hollywood.

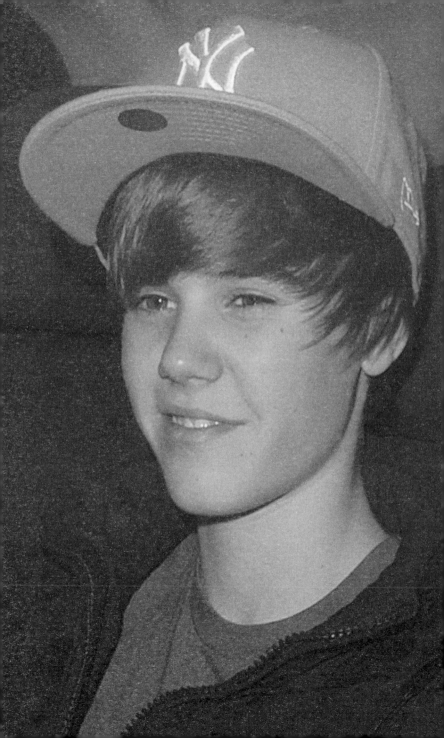

JUSTIN ENJOYED WORKING WITH FELLOW CANADIAN POP STAR AVRIL LAVIGNE ON THE 'WAVIN' FLAG' CHARITY SINGLE.

Everyone who attended was there to help celebrate what Justin, Bow Wow and other young celebrities had done for charities. There were live performances from some of the stars, pumpkin carving, great games and food too. Actor Mark Wahlberg was there with his daughters and told *Variety*: "My girls wanted to meet Justin Bieber and they came away with pictures of Justin Bieber and also with an understanding of what giving back to the community means."

As well as accepting praise for his charity work at the event Justin decided to give a special gift to the charities mentioned during the event. He tweeted afterwards: "Best part was I got to surprise the charities being honoured. My show tomorrow at the Staples Centre in LA is sold out but… We saved 500 tickets to give 100 each to each charity being honoured to give to kids in need and let them have a fun night they deserve."

That was so generous of Justin to do such a lovely thing. It would have been amazing if he had given 50 tickets away let alone 500!

Justin has been to other charity ceremonies too. He went to a special night for Usher's New Look Foundation back in August 2010. Justin told MTV on the night: "It's really important that I'm able to help out other kids. I'm a kid myself, so it means a lot to me."

Justin has also helped raise money for charity by taking part in two charity singles for the people of Haiti. Justin was so shocked when he heard about the earthquake on 12 January 2009 which killed an estimated 230,000 people. Justin wanted to help those who had been injured and made homeless by the earthquake so jumped at the chance to record 'Wavin' Flag' with other Canadian performers. He enjoyed the whole experience of uniting with people like Avril Lavigne and Nelly Furtado and was thrilled when the song went straight to the top of the Canadian music charts.

Justin didn't turn down the chance to sing on the bigger track 'We Are the World For Haiti' which featured more than 80 artists including Pink, Usher, Kanye West and the Jonas Brothers. During the mammoth recording session Justin let his fans know what was going on when he tweeted: "Singing We Are The World right now with Celine Dion next to me!! Everyone is here!! I'm meeting everyone!! This is insane! Ok ok chill."

American Idol winner Jordin Sparks also felt blessed. She tweeted: "Being a part of the We Are The World remake is such an honor. So much talent together for a great cause. I will never forget tonight."

Justin is going to be making hit records for a very,

MILEY CYRUS AND JUSTIN ARE SAID TO BE JUST FRIENDS.

very long time so he will continue to support as many charities as possible.

Crushes

Justin doesn't get nervous before performances or interviews because he has done so many of them but he does get nervous when he sees a girl he fancies. It must be hard for Justin because he is never in one place long enough to chat to a girl and get to know her. He just gets whisked off in his tour bus from one place to the next.

This means that dating a celebrity girl would be a lot easier because the girl would understand how busy Justin's schedule is and they could hang out at awards shows and other celebrity events. His fans think that any girl Justin dated would have to respect his faith because it means so much to him and also get on with his mum because they are so close. The girl couldn't be the jealous kind because Justin is always going to get attention from girls, whether he wants it or not.

In the past Justin has been linked to his friends Miley Cyrus and Taylor Swift. The rumours started because Justin enjoyed going for a meal with each of them but Justin doesn't want to date Miley or Taylor. He told *Details* magazine why he isn't interested in Taylor: "She's

JUSTIN HAS A MASSIVE CRUSH ON POP QUEEN, BEYONCÉ KNOWLES.

a little too old for me – and definitely too tall." The only member of the Cyrus family with a crush on Justin is Noah Cyrus, Miley's little sister.

The girl Justin has the biggest crush on is Beyoncé Knowles and he was gutted when she married Jay-Z. He has 'loved' her for almost 10 years and told her that she was good looking when he met her at the 2010 Grammys.

D is for...

Dad

Justin's parents were really young when he was born and they divorced when Justin was still a baby. His dad moved to Winnipeg in the Canadian province of Manitoba which was 1,700 miles away.

Justin's dad is called Jeremy Bieber and although Justin lived with his mum when he was growing up he still saw his dad when he could. They might have lived far away from each other but they still had a close relationship and Jeremy helped introduce Justin to different styles of music. Jeremy has two young children now so Justin has a half-brother and a half-sister. Jazmyn and Jaxon are too young to realise that their big brother is the biggest star on the planet, but once they get to school they will soon have people queuing up to be their friends.

Justin talked about what it was like to have divorced parents to *Seventeen* magazine: "My parents weren't the type to talk trash about each other. Some parents, when they split up, the mom will say, 'Your dad's a jerk,' but mine were never like that. So that definitely made it easier for me. I knew they loved me, and they split up because of them, not because of me."

DID YOU KNOW?

Justin's dad used to be a professional wrestler when he was younger. He now works as a carpenter and construction worker.

Justin told *Seventeen* magazine: "I have a great relationship with my dad. When I was younger, he taught me how to play some songs on the guitar, like 'Knockin' on Heaven's Door' by Bob Dylan... he's the one who got me into classic rock and then turned me on to stuff like Guns N' Roses and Metallica. He taught me how to drive too. He's cool."

OPPOSITE: JUSTIN IS ESCORTED THROUGH THE CROWDS BY HIS SECURITY GUARDS.

Jeremy has always been very proud of Justin, even before he was famous. On his official website he wrote: "My life is my son. He is nine years old and is the most talented person I know. He's a 'looker' too (just like his dad)!" He also posted up some cute photos of the two of them together but he hasn't updated the site in a long time.

Justin's love of sport and travel seems to come from his dad who describes himself as being 'very active' in his bio on the site: "I love the outdoors. I follow and play a variety of sports. I love camping and boating, but most of all, I love to travel. I've been to several countries, and hope to see the rest of the world."

Since Jeremy wrote this he has seen Justin perform in so many places, and is no doubt even prouder of him than he was when his son was just a schoolboy with a dream. If you want to follow Jeremy on Twitter you can. He posts up lovely photos of Justin sometimes and updates everyone on what he is doing. After posting a photo of Justin cuddling his brother and sister he wrote: "My lil Bieber babies… I am truly blessed to have such beautiful children!!"

Jeremy's twitter account is http://twitter.com/LordBieber and he has over 180,000 followers.

Dancing

Not only is Justin a talented singer but he is a talented dancer too. His choreographer is called Jamaica Craft. To prepare for his My World tour he practiced dancing for hours every day to make sure every routine looked perfect. He didn't want to let Jamaica or his fans down.

Jamaica is one of the most talented choreographers on the planet. She was nominated for an MTV Video Music award for best choreography in a video in 2009 for 'Love Sex Magic'. Jamaica loved working with Ciara and Justin Timberlake, who featured in the video. She had been nominated for the same award back in 2007 for another Ciara video, 'Like A Boy.' It would be great if she could win an award for one of Justin's videos. She was the choreographer behind 'Somebody to Love'.

For the tour Justin had to learn how to dance in the air wearing a safety harness but making it look like he didn't have one on. He had to appear confident at all times, no matter how high up in the sky he was.

If you want to learn to dance like Justin there are loads of good videos on YouTube that fans have made that will teach you how to do it. It will take a lot of practice though to look even half as good as Justin does when he's dancing.

When Justin is being interviewed on TV he likes teaching the presenters 'The Dougie'. The Dougie is a

dance that people do when they are really happy. You have to put your left arm up against the side of your head and then your right arm against the side of your head, with your fists clenched. You need to move your head from side to side and your arms up and down a bit (it looks like you're lifting dumbbells). Your knees need to be a bit bent and you need to move in time with the beat of the music. Justin likes doing it a lot. He has also danced The Dougie on stage with Willow Smith.

Another dance move that Justin enjoys doing is called the 'Cat Daddy'. For this dance move you have to put your left arm across the right-hand side of your body, and then your right arm across the left-hand side of your body. You then do what Justin calls a 'Wheelchair' by moving your arms in a circular movement three times down to the floor. If you want to learn this move you are best checking out a video of Justin teaching The Dougie on the *Ellen Show*.

Dating

Justin might be busy but he still finds time to date. He told *Details* magazine: "I've had girlfriends – nothing really, really serious, but I've had girlfriends. My first was when I was, like, 12 or 13. A month later, we broke up. I had that little stomach pain for a couple of days, but then I was cool."

Lots of celebrities worry about girls they have dated in the past selling stories on them to the press but none of Justin's exes have ever done that. They think he's a cool guy and know his fans would be very upset if they did. If anyone ever says something nasty about Justin on a blog or a website then fans send them negative comments and emails – and may even crash the website were the nasty post was made. Justin's fans are very protective of him.

Justin was 13 when he went on his first date and he took the lucky girl to a restaurant. Justin admitted to *M* Magazine: "If I really like a girl, I get nervous. There have been a few dates I've gone on that I was totally anxious about. I try to just stay calm and remember to be myself.

"Once I took a girl out for a first date to an Italian restaurant. During the meal I spilled spaghetti all over her! It was terrible and embarrassing. I never went out with her again. So I would suggest not going out for Italian on a first date because it can be messy! I'll never make that mistake again."

Justin might have had a bad experience in the past but he still thinks going for a meal is the best way to spend a first date. He thinks cinema dates are a bit rubbish because you can't talk properly and he much prefers getting to know a girl on a date.

Dictionary

If you have been a fan of Justin's for a while then you might recognise some of these terms from the Bieber Dictionary!

Beliebers: Fans who love Justin 100 per cent and will always be his fan – no matter what.

Biebette: The name for a single girl who is obsessed with Justin. If it is a group of girls they are called Biebettes.

Bieber-fever: Fans who love Justin so much they become obsessed with him. The only cure is a kiss from Justin.

Bieber Blast: The effect of Justin Bieber being in your town/city/country.

Bieber-Hater: People who hate Justin and say nasty things about him. They enjoy upsetting Justin's fans.

Dolls

You might not be able to hang around with the real Justin but there is now a range of Justin dolls available in shops and online. There are five Justin dolls to collect and they are each wearing an outfit from one of his music videos or that he has worn to an awards show. They play a 30-second clip of Justin singing and include a mini magazine. The company who made the dolls did a really good job because the dolls are very lifelike, unlike many other celebrity dolls.

The dolls came out just in time for Christmas 2010 and the demand was so high that some toy shops in America ran out. They couldn't cope with the thousands of fans desperate to get their hands on their own mini Justin Biebers.

The Justin Bieber Fan Club blog reported: "Toys R Us predicted demand would be so great that it flew the dolls in from Asia, rather than wait for them to arrive by boat," and that, "another company ordered 1 million dolls because they knew fans would be rushing out to get them."

UK Justin Bieber fans can order the dolls from Amazon and some other toy retailers.

A GROUP OF 'BELIEBERS' WAIT IN THE COLD TO TRY AND CATCH A
GLIMPSE OF THEIR IDOL.

Driving

Justin is used to excelling at things so it was a big shock for him when he failed his driving theory test. He was so confident that he didn't even consider he might leave the test centre without a licence.

He was so upset that he cried and walked home in the rain because he couldn't face being driven home by his mum. It was so hard for Justin because the world's media and his fans all knew how much he wanted to get behind the wheel – and he felt like a big failure.

DID YOU KNOW?
Justin only failed his test by one question.

For his second test Justin must have been more prepared and will have made sure that he read through all the questions carefully before answering them, just in case he messed up again.

Since passing his test Justin has driven some super cars. He has driven a white Lamborghini, a black Porsche and Sean Kingston's Ferrari.

The 'Beautiful Girls' hitmaker told *Popstar!* how he felt seeing Justin driving his car. He said: "I was freaking out at first, No, Bieber don't crash my car! But then I was like it's Justin Bieber so if he does crash it, he can hand over a nice cheque and I'll go buy a whole new

Ferrari, a newer one! That kid is 16. He had his permit. It was great."

Sean is a huge fan of Justin and told the magazine: "Justin is so humble and so charming! You gotta love him! My mom says she wants to pack him up in her suitcase and keep him! Nah, he's a good dude. That's my little brother, man."

Duets

Justin is so popular and talented that people are lining up to do duets with him. He has such a unique singing voice. Usher featured on 'First Dance' with Justin, Ludacris featured on 'Baby', Jessica Jarrell featured on 'Overboard', Sean Kingston featured on 'Eenie Meenie' and Jaden Smith featured on 'Never Say Never'. He would love it if Beyoncé did a duet with him as she is the person he would most like to do a duet with in the whole world.

Now it looks like Justin will be recording a track with country band Rascal Flatts. They are a big band in the USA and have released seven studio albums and five compilation albums over the last 20 years. Their lead singer Gary LeVox told WSIX: "[Justin] asked us to do a duet with him on his next record, It's actually a really good song!" Justin will be recording the single in

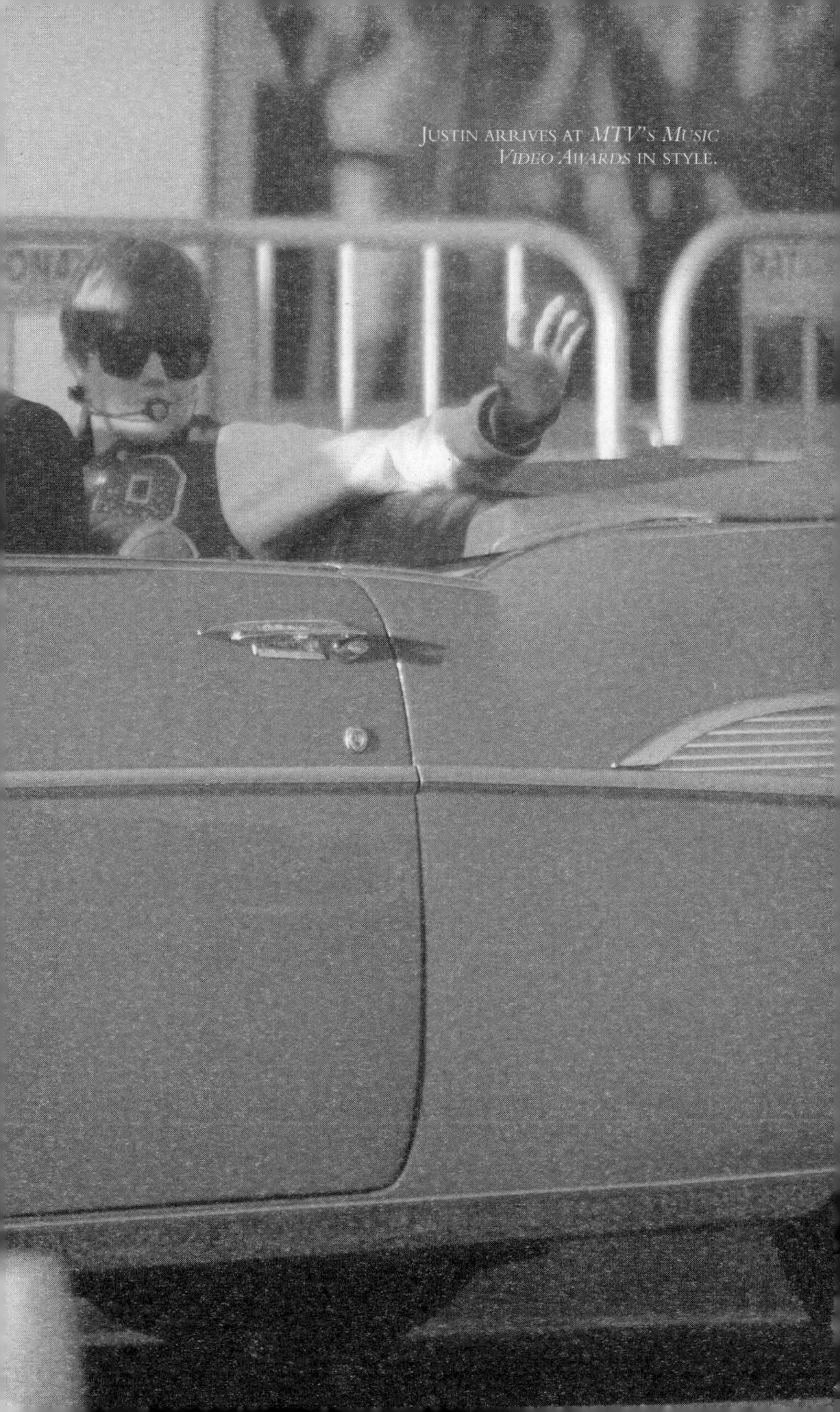

Justin arrives at *MTV's Music Video Awards* in style.

Nashville, which is seen as the home of country music by many people.

Demi Lovato really wants to do a duet with Justin and Miley Cyrus. She revealed to one reporter: "We're talking a long time about the possibility of doing a duet together, and in particular it would be something acoustic.

"He's very sweet. I like to work with him. My sister loves him and I am a fan of his, in fact I can say that I have Justin Fever!"

Justin has already had the opportunity to work with one star that you wouldn't necessarily pair him with. He has been in the studio recording with top hip-hop producer Dr. Dre. They haven't decided to release the track they worked on in July or discussed it in any great detail but Justin did tweet at the time: "Got to be in the studio with the legend himself Dr. Dre… made a couple beats and he gave me some advice. I was hyped. can u blame me?"

In December 2010 Justin's fans had confirmation that Justin would be releasing a song in the new year with Chris Brown. Fans had a feeling it was going to happen because Justin tweeted a video of him singing Chris Brown's classic track 'With You' in October with the message: "Kinda hyped (right) now for a new single teamed up with one of my friends and

POP STARLET JESSICA JARRELL FEATURED ON JUSTIN'S TRACK, 'OVERBOARD'.

FRIEND AND MENTOR LUDACRIS DUETED WITH JUSTIN ON 'BABY'.

an artist I used to sing covers of on YouTube. BIG RECORD. SMASH!!"

It was confirmed when Chris Brown tweeted: "ME and @justinbieber got a BANGER/SMASH record for all the fans out there at the top of the NEW YEAR!!! 2011."

E is for...

Exercise

You don't get to be as fit as Justin without working out. He might only be small but he still puts time in at the gym. He has his own personal trainer who looks after him and makes sure he doesn't do too much or too little.

According to reports, Justin's personal trainer is called Jordan Yuam. Justin isn't the first celebrity that Jordan has trained, he also looks after Taylor Lautner and helped him transform his body for *New Moon*. Jordan is a firm believer that if you want to get fitter then exercise isn't enough, you have to change your diet too.

It's thought that Justin and Jordan work out hundreds of miles apart from each other when Justin is on the road by going on Skype. Justin is supposed to have changed his diet too and replaced burgers for avocados but there has been no official word from his spokesperson.

Justin has always loved sport so probably finds kicking a football around or going for a swim the best form of exercise. He can't go jogging around the block like a normal teenager would do because he would get mobbed by fans and paparazzi. He can't do too much work in the gym either because his body is still growing and he could cause himself some damage if he overtrained.

Being on tour with professional dancers must help Justin exercise more than he would do at home because he can join in with what they are doing. In order to be able to put on a show every night Justin needs to be super fit.

F is for...

Facebook

Justin has an official Facebook page with almost 19 million fans! There are lots of imposters out there but there is only one real Justin Bieber on Facebook.

Justin has seven favourite pages on Facebook and they include those on his best celebrity friends and charities he supports: Usher, Taylor Swift, Asher Roth, Pencils of Promise, Make-A-Wish Foundation of America, Children's Miracle Network and Praying for Hayley Okines.

Hayley Okines is a huge fan of Justin and suffers from a disease called progeria. The disease is extremely rare and only 53 people in the whole world are thought to have it. Hayley is only 13 but she suffers from baldness, heart problems and arthritis, conditions that normally affect pensioners. The average life span of someone with the disease is 13 so Hayley's friends did all they could to try and make her wish to meet Justin come true. After setting up the Facebook page and the twitter account BiebsmeetHayley Hayley's friends managed to get in touch with Justin's friend Christian and he told Justin all about Hayley and her wish.

Justin arranged to meet Hayley in December 2010 but it was a secret. He tweeted: "About to meet someone very special soon."

Later on he sent the following messages to Hayley's friends who arranged for her to meet him:

@BiebsmeetHayley u did a good thing. and you were right she has a great smile. :)
@BiebsmeetHayley it was actually kinda funny. she had no clue and when she saw me she screamed and everyone was like what the?!?! lol
@BiebsmeetHayley she was real sweet and i offered her tix for the show in the UK when im back. i think you should go with her then too
This is when we first saw each other in the lobby

after THE SCREAM! :) thanks for introducing us. she is a sweet girl http://twitpic.com/3d6edh @BiebsmeetHayley like i said…u and the fans did a good thing. glad i could help.

It's lovely that Justin took time out of his busy schedule to meet Hayley and by adding her page to his favourite pages he was showing his fans that he cared for her and asking them to pray for her too.

On Justin's Facebook fan page you can sign up for newsletters and view some great photos of Justin that you won't have seen before. You can also discuss Justin with other fans but be aware that some people go on the discussion boards just to say nasty things about him and aren't genuine fans at all. Never leave your phone number or personal info on a discussion board, the wall or anywhere else online because it could get into the wrong hands.

Justin used to have a 'Stories' tab on his Facebook page but he had to remove it after it caused huge problems. Justin didn't realise what would happen when he tweeted: "Good morning world… just added the new STORIES tab to my facebook page. Its for u to share ur stories and adventures about how myself or my music is in ur life."

He thought he would get a few fans leaving messages

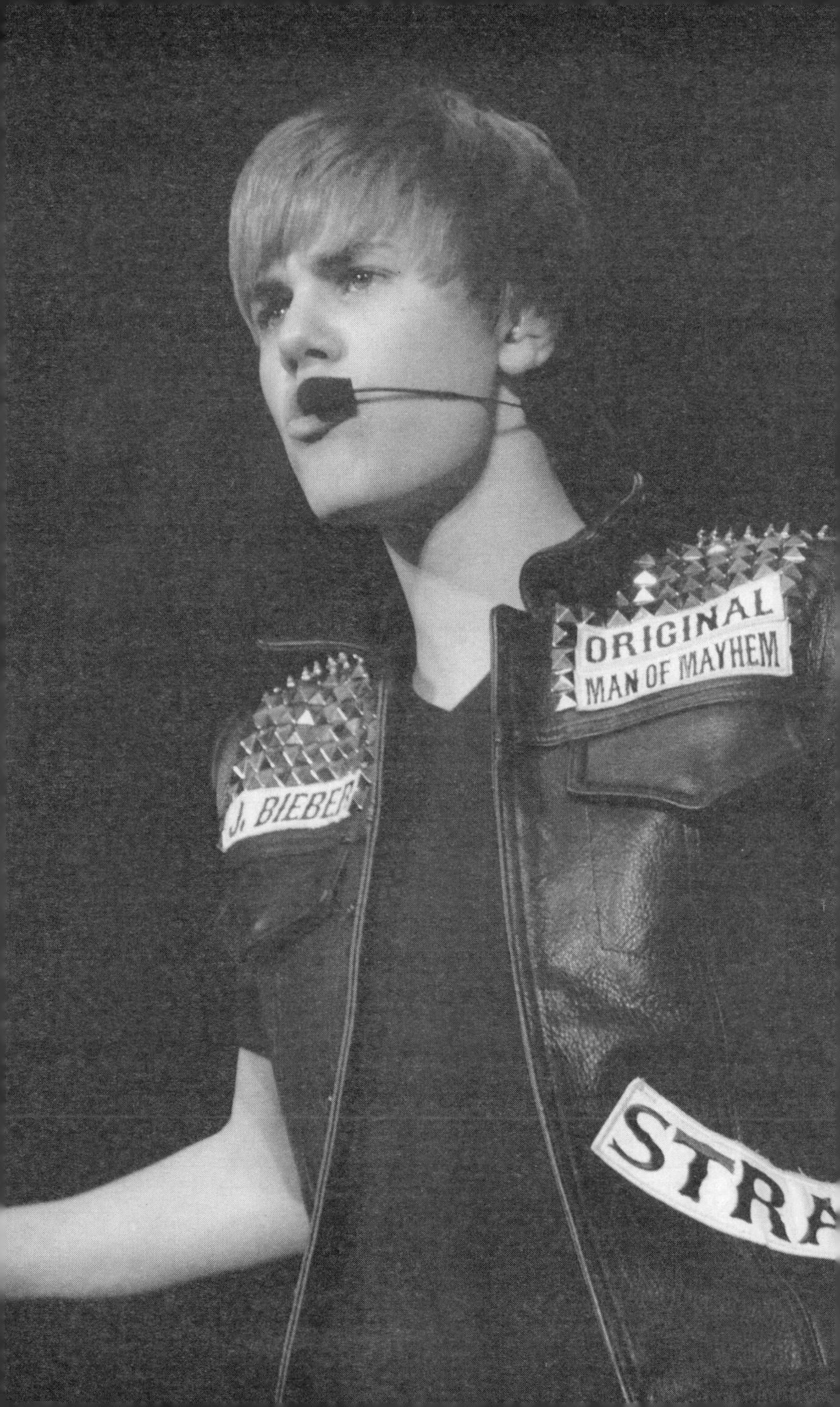
ORIGINAL
MAN OF MAYHEM
J. BIEBER

but he never expected to get as many as he did in such a short space of time. Only one hour after he posted his message the tab had to be removed. Justin explained to fans: "WOW- facebook had to remove the STORIES Tab from my page for now because it was crashing the system!!! hahaha…I LOVE MY FANS!!"

In July 2010 *The Huffington Post* published a list of the Top 50 Most Popular People on Facebook. Justin made it into the top 10, with approximately 50,000 new people joining his fan page a day.

THE TOP TEN:

1. Michael Jackson
2. Lady Gaga
3. Vin Diesel
4. Barack Obama
5. Megan Fox
6. Cristiano Ronaldo
7. Hugh Laurie
8. Lil Wayne
9. Justin Bieber
10. Taylor Swift

Since then Justin has overtaken Lil Wayne, Hugh Laurie, Cristiano Ronaldo and Barack Obama so is sitting in fifth place. It is only a matter of time before he's in the top three. We will have to wait and see if he ever beats the legend that is Michael Jackson.

Fame

Justin is determined to stay grounded. He thinks his mum, his friends and his faith in God will help him. He wants to still be performing and making hit records in 10, 20 years' time. His mum often travels with him which helps him keep his feet on the ground.

Being famous does have its disadvantages when Justin just wants to enjoy a quiet meal out with his family and friends. He gets recognised in so many countries now because he is a global superstar. When he went out for dinner in the Indian restaurant La Porte Indes in London on 2 December he had a drawn-on moustache which made him look at least ten years older than he actually is. He took a toy helicopter with him too which must have made him stand out from the other diners.

When he went out for a meal in New York he wore a trench coat, hat and glasses but people still recognised the small bit of his face that was on show. Photographers took photos but Justin didn't stop to chat as he was on his way to meet Rihanna. When Justin goes for lunch or dinner with a fellow celeb he gets followed by even more

photographers than usual because they want to snap a photo of Justin and his new girlfriend (even though Justin isn't dating them).

Justin has done amazingly well to have become so famous in such a short period of time. He was asked by the host of *The Today Show* how he managed it because he didn't have the backing of Disney or Nickelodeon, as Miley Cyrus and the Jonas Brothers do. Justin replied: "Basically I just thought, you know, I'm just going to make good music and not really limit myself to any sort of crowd. I know lots of teenagers do like me but I just kinda wanna reach everybody. I don't want to limit myself."

Sometimes fame can get too much for Justin and he says things he doesn't mean. He might be feeling tired or homesick but he still has to do interviews sometimes. When a journalist, Liz Jones interviewed him he had lost his voice but he still had to answer all her questions. She asked him about his fans and how much they love him. He replied: "It is not real love. You can say it is, but it's not. They do not know who I am." Justin also admitted that he feels lonely despite his millions of fans: "I want to hang out with my friends, but I need security. I'm going to get my dog to come on the road in a couple of weeks."

Being famous means that your words can get twisted

and appear out of context so what you said looks worse than it is. The day before his interview with Liz Jones he tweeted: "U know u wake up and you go online sometimes and see your words twisted or isolated from the whole meaning. It is frustrating... you become guarded.

"Sometimes u dont know who to trust. U say one thing to someone and it comes out totally different... that is why i like twitter. i can say it how it is. no one twisting things."

DID YOU KNOW?

If Justin hadn't become a singer he would have liked to have been an architect because he has always enjoyed drawing. Although he probably wouldn't have liked the seven years of training he would have had to do to become qualified. Being an architect takes so much hard work and dedication.

He would also quite like to be a chef. He told one journalist: "If I wasn't a pop star I'd be a chef... I'd cook all the lovely ladies a nice dinner."

Family

Justin has a huge extended family and they are all so proud of him. His grandpa in particular gets so emotional when he sees Justin on stage.

Some of Justin's extended family are French Canadian and don't speak English so Justin learnt French so he could speak to them. He is fluent and added a French version of 'One Less Lonely Girl' on the Canadian version of *My World*. He also sang in French for his French fans when he was performing in Paris – that was a cool experience.

DID YOU KNOW?

His great grandfather was German and immigrated to Canada.

Family means everything to Justin and if he had to choose between his family or music he would pick his family because they mean so much to him.

Justin might be more than ten years older than his little sister Jazmyn and brother Jaxon but they have a really close bond. They might live in Canada but to Justin the distance isn't a problem because he can just hop on a plane and go visit them when he has a few days off.

On 30th May Justin proved to his fans how much his

JUSTIN GETS THE
CROWD GOING
DURING A LIVE
PERFORMANCE.

family means to him when he tweeted: "family is always a top priority….2day is my lil sis bday….told everyone i couldnt make it….then put on my disguise and SURPRISE!! haha SURPRISE JAZZY- I couldnt let u celebrate 2 alone…even surprised my jaxon. lol"

Justin then posted a cute photo of little Jaxon with the caption, 'My baby bro chillin ☺'.

Justin, Jazmyn and Jaxon share the same dad but have different mums. Justin's mum is Pattie and Jazmyn and Jaxon's mum is called Erin. She is Jeremy's second wife.

Pattie didn't have any other children after Justin which turned out to be a good thing because she can travel with Justin wherever he goes. If she had other children she might have had to stay at home and look after them.

Fan Mail

Justin loves receiving fan mail and gifts from his fans. If you want to write to him or want an autograph then you need to send a self-addressed envelope to his fan mail address. If you want a photo signing then it is best to send the photo with your letter. It can take a few months to hear back but sometimes Justin replies after a month. It just depends how busy he is at the time he receives your letter.

The address you need:

Justin Bieber
c/o Island Def Jam Group
Worldwide Plaza
825 8th Ave
28th Floor
New York, NY 10019
USA

Justin is overwhelmed by the amazing presents he receives from fans. They spend time picking the perfect present or sometimes make unique gifts just for him.

Justin's favourite ever present was probably his dog tag. He explained to *BOP!* "A fan actually gave it to me... It was someone very special to them that had passed away in the war and this was his dog tag. I wear it for the fans."

Justin was blown away when he found out the story behind the dog tag and felt blessed that the fan had given it to him. He spends hours at a time looking through his fan mail, signing autographs and opening his presents from fans. He really likes the scrapbooks that fans make which include lots of photos, messages and mementos. Justin has some very talented fans who draw amazing pictures for him. He

Justin flashes his
amazing smile.

Justin poses for photos outside the MTV Music Awards in 2010.

Justin inflicts 'Bieber
Fever' at the Jingle Bell
Ball in New Jersey.

Above: Justin meets his fans in Germany.

Below left: Justin performs on stage in Miami in 2010.

Below right: He says 'hi' to a 'Biebette' during a live performance.

Two of the most important people of Justin's career: mentor Usher (*above*) and his beloved mother Pattie (*below*).

Above: Justin arrives for the premiere of *Megamind* in October 2010.

Below: Mr Bieber smiles for the cameras prior to going on the David Letterman show.

gets hundreds of letters every day which must make Justin feel very loved and lift his spirits on days when he isn't 100 per cent happy.

DID YOU KNOW?

Justin's grandmother still lives in Stratford and ends up getting a few fan letters addressed to Justin every week. A spokesperson from Canada Post told her local paper *The Star*: "He's getting maybe a couple pieces of mail a week. It's coming to 'Justin Bieber, Stratford, Canada' or 'Stratford, Ontario'.

"That is not a correct address, but these are interesting circumstances and heck, we have some cognizance of the pop culture at Canada Post, along with everybody else and so do our employees... because of the size of the community, we have an idea who is who – a pop icon who is from this part of the country, with known relatives; we're playing along a little bit for this one."

Fans

Justin's fans are some of the most dedicated in the world. They will follow Justin no matter what. Back in October 2009 Justin discussed his fans with *Details* magazine. He said: "I met a six-month-old baby. I've got

FANS SHOW THEIR LOVE FOR THEIR FAVOURITE POP STAR.

some young fans, but the majority of them are like 14, 15. My mom's like 35, so she's my oldest fan.

"I don't mind it (when fans flash their bras). Just kidding – it's not something that's cool for them to do. There was this one girl in Seattle – I didn't even see her – she runs at me, tries to give me a hug and tackles me. It was really aggressive and scary."

His fans will even fight between themselves sometimes. During a concert in Pittsburgh Justin threw a towel into the audience and two girls started scrapping over it. Justin ended up having to stop singing mid-song and ask them to stop.

Every time Justin performs 'One Less Lonely Girl' he serenades one lucky fan from the audience. The girls are often overcome with emotion and feel like they are dreaming. One of his chosen girls spoke to Canada AM about her perfect moment with Justin.

Fourteen-year-old Emma Curto admitted: "When he touched my face, that just made my life."

Emma had just been enjoying the concert when someone approached her and asked if she wanted to be the 'One Less Lonely Girl'. There were 15,000 people watching but Emma was the one they picked that night. "I was just sitting in my seat and I had no idea that this was going to happen... I was all pumped and I was like, 'All right, I am going to make the most

of this. I only get to do this once.'" Emma's dad was a bit worried at one point in the song because he thought Justin was going to kiss her. He added: "It looked like he was getting close enough for a kiss. Right at that point, they just touched heads, and I was kind of grateful."

It's a good job Justin doesn't kiss the fans chosen for this song because the girls would never be able to get over the fact that they kissed Justin Bieber. It was hard enough for Emma having to leave the stage with her bouquet of red roses – if he had kissed her she might have fainted!

Since returning home Emma has framed her concert ticket with a photo of Justin. She knows she will treasure her time with Justin forever. She ended the interview saying: "It is the best memory of my life. It will be the best moment of my life. Nothing can top that, unless we get married."

Justin loves all of his fans equally but he thinks that fans in different countries behave differently to reach him. He thinks his Thai fans are more reserved than his USA and UK fans, as they give him space. Some fans are willing to do whatever it takes to get close to Justin. One mum from Miami had a radio show presenter's face tattooed on her back so she could win backstage tickets to meet Justin.

When journalist Tim Aylen asked him which country has the most vocal fans Justin answered: "I think my home country, Canada, has the most vocal fans. It feels unbelievable when I go home to feel such love. It's amazing whenever I get that kind of support, but to be able to connect with my fellow Canadians is awesome!"

Most fans cry, scream or faint when they meet Justin. He doesn't understand why they react in extreme ways.

In a recent interview with Contact Music he confessed: "I'm not even that cool, like seriously. What is so cool that you freak out? These girls crying, it's like I can't believe that, I'm so honoured that you're crying but, I don't know, it's crazy to me!"

Justin has quite a unique name but there is a 35-year-old man from Florida who shares his name with our favourite singer. He has had fans ring him up wanting to speak to Justin – at all hours of the day and night. He ended up putting his wife's name in the phone book to try and stop it happening but someone posted his phone number up on a fan site. He has had to unplug his phone because he can get over a hundred messages in just a few days. He even gets fan mail.

The older Justin was banned from Facebook because the site thought he was an imposter, even though it is his real name. He says they just deleted his account one day without any warning. Hopefully things will get sorted soon and fans will stop hassling him and instead write to Justin at his official fan mail address instead.

Our favourite Justin loves spending time with his fans and posing for photos but he doesn't like it when fans are too nervous. He told *Teen Vogue* what advice he would like to offer these nervous fans. He said: "Just talk to me. Ask me how I'm doing. Introduce yourself instead of yelling, 'Justin! Justin! Justin! Can I have a picture?' And don't come up to me while I'm eating. How would you like it if I came into your house and started taking pictures of you while you were eating? I hate that."

Sometimes fans can get overexcited and put Justin's life at risk. When Justin flew into a New Zealand airport in April 2010 he had no idea that he was about to be mobbed by his fans. He was surrounded by them and had to rush out of the airport as fast as he could before things turned nasty. His mum was knocked to the floor and someone stole the hat from his head, which shows how crazy the fans were. Everyone just got caught up in the moment and no fan set out to upset Justin or his mum.

Justin tweeted afterwards: "Finally got to New Zealand last night. The airport was crazy. Not happy that someone stole my hat and knocked down my mama. Come on people. I want to be able to sign and take pics and meet my fans, but if you are all pushing security won't let me. Let's keep it safe and have fun."

Justin's fans who heard that his mum had been knocked over were worried for her and sent her messages of support. She soon tweeted them back a thank you message: "Thanks for all ur support!! I'm ok thank you!!!"

The girls who had stolen Justin's hat had been hoping that Justin would agree to meet them in person and give them a hug each. They saw it as an opportunity to meet him but he wasn't prepared to give in to their demands. He gave a journalist from 3 News a message to pass on to them: "You stole my property. It's essentially illegal. But, it's fine, I forgive you... I love you." The girls ended up returning the hat but must have been gutted that their plan didn't work.

Justin later tweeted: "Sorry, you can't hold me to ransom... I got my hat back. No hugs, no thanks u's. Just glad they did the right thing. I don't condone thievery!! Haha."

It's a good job that Justin didn't meet the girls because if he had it would have encouraged more fans to pull similar stunts in the future. He needs to feel safe and secure when he is out and about, and not feel worried that people are going to steal things from him.

Justin wants all his fans to keep dreaming big dreams. Sometimes people can say that fans who dream of meeting Justin face to face are silly because there is no chance of it happening. Justin would disagree because anything is possible. He was just a schoolboy in Stratford one day and the next he was hanging out with Usher.

Fascinating Facts

TAKE A LOOK AT THIS LIST OF FASCINATING FACTS ABOUT JUSTIN...

- Justin can complete a Rubik cube in one-and-a half minutes. The world record is 6.77 seconds so he's still got a way to go if he is to break it one day.
- Justin took part in the milk challenge and managed to drink a pint of milk in 26.03 seconds. He loves challenges and will try almost anything.
- Justin did one of the scariest things a person can do when he bungee-jumped off a bridge in New Zealand.
- He has a dog called Sam who is a Papillon. Justin says Sam is his best friend and he helped him cope when he moved to Atlanta.

Food

Justin is quite experimental when it comes to food and he likes to try new dishes when he is visiting a new country. He might not always like the taste of something but the important thing is that he isn't afraid to try something he hasn't tried before. He has eaten in some top best restaurants over the last two years but never seems to have a problem getting a table. He isn't very keen on English food but likes Italian, especially spaghetti bolognese and pizza. His favourite dessert is apple pie and in the mornings he likes to have Cap'n Crunch cereal.

Justin loves sweets so, so, much and likes to eat Sour Patch Kids and Gummy Worms just before he performs. They must give him lots of energy. Sour Patch Kids are sour tasting chewy sweets that come in five flavours in an average pack. They were launched in the USA in 1985 but have yet to reach the UK. Gummy Worms are loved all over the world, so Justin never really needs to go without them. His favourite fast food place is Subway.

Many fans were shocked when Justin and his team's tour rider was revealed online. It stated that they ate around 10,000 fries a day and drank approximately 75 Starbucks' beverages between them. Justin does have a huge team though, so it's not as if he sat and ate all the fries himself!

When Justin is due to appear on a TV show he is often asked what he would like in his dressing room and he picks simple things like fruit platters and bottles of mineral water. He isn't a diva like other celebrities who are famous for asking for kittens, doves or for the room to be redecorated just for them.

> **DID YOU KNOW?**
>
> Justin wants to date someone who can cook because he can't!

Football

Justin is a huge football fan and has been playing since he was very young. In Canada they call the sport soccer rather than football but Justin can use both terms in interviews. If you go on YouTube you can see a video of Justin showing off his football skills before he was famous. He played for a local team called the Stratford Strikers. They were a travel soccer team and played their home matches on the Cooper Standard Soccer Fields. Justin loved scoring goals for the team and travelling to matches in the bus all together. His crew on his tour have kind of replaced

OPPOSITE: JUSTIN LOVES TO EAT SWEETS – ESPECIALLY 'GUMMY WORMS' – BEFORE HE PERFORMS ON STAGE.

the football team but Justin still remembers the good times. He actually mentions the Stratford Strikers in his first album sleeve along with the other people he wanted to thank for making him the person he is today.

Justin supports Chelsea but his favourite player is Wayne Rooney, even though the guy plays for Manchester United. He would love it if David Beckham would give him football lessons, and has offered to do a private concert for him and his family in return. We will just have to wait and see if Justin gets his wish.

Justin told *The Sun*: "I am sure he would do anything to make his three boys happy and if I am their favourite artist I would happily come and put on a private show at the Beckham household.

"All I would ask for in return is that we go into his yard for an hour afterward and he teaches me all those crazy things he can do with a soccer ball."

Justin might have a packed schedule but he still likes to watch football on TV when he can. In the summer of 2010 he made sure he watched the final of the World Cup. He tweeted: "who do u guys think is gonna win this World Cup Final?? looking like a good game."

Once the match finished Justin wanted to

congratulate Spain on beating the Netherlands 1-0. "wow…SPAIN!! great game…nothing to be ashamed of. True champions on both sides. Congrats to Spain," he tweeted.

G is for...

Girlfriends

If you would love to date Justin then you might be interested to find out what he looks for in a potential girlfriend. He prefers girls who are naturally beautiful and confessed to MTV: "I don't like girls who wear lots of make-up and you can't see their face. Some girls are beautiful but insecure and look much better without the make-up, but decide to put loads on. I like girls with nice eyes and a nice smile." He isn't a fan of Ugg boots or huge, round sunglasses but isn't too fussy about whether the girl is a blond, brunette or redhead.

Justin likes girls who are funny, confident and outgoing.

He prefers girls who are true to themselves and don't pretend to be something they're not. He doesn't just want a girlfriend who looks good, he wants one with brains too as he explained to German newspaper *BILD*: "It would be a shame to go out with a hot girl you can't have a decent conversation with!"

Justin wouldn't mind having a girlfriend who was older than him – and has even hinted that he'd date someone up to the age of 40. It would be very weird if he did though, because she'd be older than his mum.

If Justin spots a girl that he wants to ask out on a date he plays it cool and doesn't come out and ask her straight away. He said to *Top of the Pops* magazine: "It depends on the situation. But at first I won't let her know – you've got to pace yourself. Then, maybe by the end of the conversation, I'd ask her something like, 'Do you have a phone number that I could reach you at?' That's usually how it goes."

Most celebrities have two mobiles, one for their close friends and family, and the other for people they don't know very well. If the new people they have trusted to give their mobile number to betray their trust and give it out then the celebrity can just get a new phone or number, without having to change their main phone.

Justin might be single now but he does date. His mum didn't want him to at first because she didn't think he was mature enough to have a girlfriend. She thought it would be better if he waited a few years but it wasn't to be. Justin loves girls too much!

It is hard for celebrities to know whether the person they are dating genuinely likes them or if they are only interested in them because they are famous and have lots of money. That's why many celebrities end up dating other celebrities.

Justin actually admitted in September 2010 that he is trying to stay single. Having a girlfriend complicates things when you are as busy as Justin. He is so tied up jetting all over the place that it would be hard to maintain a relationship with someone, unless the girl travelled with him.

That said, Justin would still like to get to know *Harry Potter* actress Emma Watson better. He admitted in an interview with *The Sun*: "I would love to take her out for dinner. It would be great if she could come to one of my concerts, then we could hang out afterward. I love the fact she is one of the biggest female movie stars, but has chosen to go back to college. It shows she is really grounded and normal."

He also thinks dating Cheryl Cole or Katy Perry would be cool. He divulged to *OK!* magazine: "Cheryl Cole and Katy Perry are two of the hottest girls in the world – and so normal and funny with it. If I was a few

Justin would love to get to know *Harry Potter* star Emma Watson.

years older, they are the kind of girls I'd like to date. I want a younger version of Cheryl and Katy – a mixture of the two would be hot."

Even though they are too old for him he would like to take them out for a meal so they can give him dating tips and help him find a girlfriend as nice as them.

Justin might date a fan in the future but for now he is concentrating on his music. Usher actually warned Justin off dating fans because he knows what it is like and how it can mess things up. He told *Music Time*: "I tell Justin you've got to love all your fans without falling in love with them. I can't say I've never dated a fan but it's not a good idea. I tell him to understand that you are a fantasy to them and you should be mindful of that.

"And I encourage him to not take success so seriously so early. Have fun with it. And make friends!"

Justin can't go on normal dates because the paparazzi follow him everywhere he goes. When he wanted to go on a date with Selena Gomez he had to pretend that he had just bumped into her. He went to see a high school football game with Jaden and Will Smith, and Selena 'accidentally' ended up sitting next to him. Justin must find it hard that he has to be careful all the time and isn't able to just date like any other teenager.

Justin might not have had a long-term, serious relationship yet but he still dreams about settling down and getting married. In the next 10 years he would like to find his Mrs Bieber and have kids.

DID YOU KNOW?

One night Justin was sleeping over at his mate's house and some girls texted them. It was 3am but Justin and his mate decided to sneak out and go and meet up with them. They didn't get far though, cops spotted them and took them back to the house. Justin's mum was furious and grounded him for a month.

Justin did dump a girlfriend over the phone once but he regrets it now. It wasn't the right way to do it, he should have done it in person really. Justin hasn't named the girl but they had been dating for seven months.

He told *Top of the Pops* magazine: "I have dumped a girl over the phone – it's terrible isn't it? We got into an argument during a phone call so I basically said, 'I don't wanna be with you any more,' and she cried. I saw her after that and it was a bit awkward, but we're not enemies now, so that's cool.

"But I wouldn't recommend it, it's very mean!"

Justin has grown up a lot since then and is much more romantic. He isn't a guy that likes to buy flowers and chocolates for a girl, instead he likes to be romantic in his actions. He will open doors, take her for a meal in a nice restaurant, walk her to her front door – he is the perfect gentleman.

Any girl that Justin dates must get on with his mum and understand that Pattie is always going to be Justin's number one. When it's Valentine's Day Justin likes to show his mum how much she means to him.

He told the *New York Post*: "I have one person that I'll be sending flowers to and that's my mom. She's been there since the beginning and has given up a lot for me, I'm very blessed to have her. She likes roses, so I think I might send her the 'One Less Lonely Girl' bouquet."

DID YOU KNOW?

Justin had his first crush on a girl when he was 13 and still living in Canada. He plucked up enough courage to ask her out but she said no. She must be kicking herself now because she could be dating the biggest star on the planet right at this moment.

God

Justin is so thankful to God every single day and unlike other stars who think their success is all down to

Opposite: Justin has a strong faith.

themselves he knows that he wouldn't be anything without God.

He told journalist Jon Ronson: "I pray all the time. I pray two to three times a day. When I wake up I thank him for my blessings. I thank him for putting me in this position. And at the end of the day I get out my Bible. At home-school my tutor is Christian, so we go over Bible verses. It's something that keeps me grounded."

Having a faith in God and Jesus helps Justin when he is having a bad day as he can talk to God about it. He prays and reads his Bible. It must help that his mum, his tutor and lots of his crew are Christians because he can talk to them about God and pray with them. He can also pray with Scooter who is Jewish and before he performs on his tour everyone behind the scenes comes together and stands in a prayer circle.

Justin never hides his faith from his fans and asks them to pray alongside him. He believes that prayer changes things and when there was an earthquake in Indonesia he tweeted about it. He has also asked fans to pray for celebrities facing tough times and for normal people too.

H is for...

Hair

Everyone loves Justin's hair and it is a big talking point in the press. In November 2010 he only brushed his hair to the opposite side to normal and people went crazy, thinking that he had done something drastically different to his hair.

Scooter tweeted: "…he brushes his hair in the opposite direction and the whole world thinks he has a hair cut. no haircut. just needs to shake his head."

"feel like @justinbieber 's hair brushed in opposite directions is like Clark Kent w/ glasses. Simple but the whole world cant figure it out"

JUSTIN'S HAIR HAS
BECOME A WORLDWIDE
PHENOMENON.

His fans might love his hair but Justin wouldn't mind if he didn't have any and has even considered shaving it all off. He fancies having a new hairstyle but thinks that he would be best leaving it as it is for a while.

Some people like to joke that Justin is like Samson from the Bible whose strength was in his hair. Once he had his hair cut he lost all his power. When Selena Gomez was being interviewed by MTV she was asked if Justin's power was in his hair. She replied: "I don't think it's the hair, I don't.

"Everybody wants to cut his hair. I want to cut his hair! You're with him and you have, like, a 45-second conversation and it's like [flicking his hair all the time] and I'm like, 'Why are you doing that!'

"I don't think it's the hair, I don't. He's got game. He knows what he's doing. Yes, he does. He knows exactly what he's doing. He's a very sweet kid and he loves his fans, and I think that's why he is Justin Bieber."

Megan Fox is a big fan of Justin's hair and told *E! News*: "He's got more talent in those bangs than I've got in my whole body."

Justin's hair might look great but it is really low maintenance. He just jumps in the shower, dries it by shaking his head from side to side and he's ready to go. He doesn't have to style it with gel or anything.

At the local barber shop in Stratford, close to where

Justin used to hang out with his mates, 30 boys a week ask to have their hair cut like Justin's. Some even ask for their hair to be dyed the same colour as Justin's because they love his hair so much.

DID YOU KNOW?

Justin does have bad hair days. Before he became a global superstar he went and had his hair cut into a different style to normal. His mum filmed him singing Chris Brown's 'With You' and posted it on YouTube. His hair might not have looked good but his followers didn't seem to mind. They loved his performance regardless and it became his most successful video up until that point – with a million views! Now all his home videos have been viewed millions of times but the 'With You' video is very special because it was the first to reach that milestone.

Highlights

Justin's highlights so far have been presenting at the Grammys, meeting Barack Obama and finding out he had a number one album. 2010 was an awesome year for Justin but 2011 is going to be even better!

Another highlight for Justin was hearing one of his

songs played on the radio for the first time. Justin was in the car with his mum and he was changing channels when he heard his voice. His mum made him turn it up so it was loud. They enjoyed it for a few seconds and then Justin changed channels again. He must have heard his music on the radio hundreds of times now, in different countries too.

Justin loves his life and wouldn't change it for the world.

Hockey

Justin is a huge hockey fan! He has always loved watching matches live and on TV. Loving hockey is part of being Canadian. He has supported the Toronto Maple Leafs since he was tiny and played for some local teams with his mates. He might have been small but he was fast. He also supported his local adult team 'the Cullitons'.

Justin started playing for the house hockey league but when he got too old he started playing for the travel hockey team in Stratford. They played their games at the William Allman Memorial Arena on Morenz Drive.

Justin's big hockey hero when he was growing up was Wayne Gretzky. Wayne had the nickname 'The Great One' and is regarded as the best hockey player there has ever been. He played for several teams over the years but ended his career with The New York Rangers in 1999.

Justin told a journalist: "I was never the kid that was, like, 'Oh, I want to be famous,' or, 'I want to be out there.'

"I sang, but it was just for fun... I did a lot of different stuff. I played sports. Singing was just another hobby... And I never took it seriously. I never got lessons.

"I use to practise my signature for hockey. It's kind of how I learned to give my autograph."

Justin's best mates Ryan and Chaz wanted to be professional hockey players too. Maybe it's appropriate that Justin's first concert of his My World Tour took place at the XL Center in Hartford where the Connecticut Whale AHL hockey team play their matches. Justin must have dreamt of playing hockey at big arenas and he kind of half managed to fulfil his dream but instead of playing hockey he was singing to thousands of people.

Holidays

Justin's best ever holiday was his first proper break with just himself and his mum. He had managed to save up enough money from busking over the summer to take his mum to Disney World in Florida. Justin had not long been signed by Scooter when they went, which no doubt made it more special because they knew things were about to change.

Performing all around the world is great but sometimes Justin just needs a break. He doesn't get time off very often so when he does he likes to pop back to Canada to see his little brother and sister or go on holiday somewhere hot. Justin loves hitting the beach and messing around in the sea.

Sometimes Justin will stick around in a country after he has performed there so he can have a nice holiday and see more of the country. He enjoyed performing and holidaying in Hawaii in October 2010. He tweeted a photo of a cake he was given and also said: "Sick day out on the boat with the whole crew. little jack johnson playing and some sunshine and some sea turtles and dolphins. Great day."

Justin was joined on holiday by Jaden Smith and Jasmine Villegas. Many people suspected at the time that Justin was dating Jasmine. She had been his love interest in the video for 'Baby' and they had been seen out together a few times. Jaden and Jasmine flew there just to spend some quality time with Justin. Justin, Jaden and Jasmine enjoyed going on a catamaran and hanging out in the sunshine. In the evening Jaden joined Justin on stage and they sang their hit 'Never Say Never' to the excited Hawaiian audience.

Jaden Smith and Justin are good friends and dueted on their hit-single, 'Never Say Never'.

Justin does miss his fans when he's on holiday, even though he's having lots of fun. He tweeted: "Hawaii great night and great vacation here. me, jaden, and @JASMINEVILLEGAS all had a great time. thank u. cant wait to come back!!"

Justin loves going on holiday to tropical places the most, especially the Bahamas. Justin doesn't like quiet, relaxing holidays, he likes mad, fun-packed vacations. He wants to try new things, play sport on the beach, go swimming with dolphins.

He told journalist Tim Aylen what his must-have holiday items are: "My iPod definitely. My laptop, because I'm constantly making music, and I can communicate with my friends." Justin also needs his mobile so he can keep in touch with everyone.

His favourite cities to visit (apart from Atlanta and Stratford) are Los Angeles, Sydney and Tokyo. He loved visiting Tokyo in April 2010. He tweeted when he was over there: "only been here a little while and Tokyo is already 1 of my favorite cities.

"Exclusive kicks everywhere..great food..and heated toilet seats"

"just had sushi dinner here in Japan. food was incredible but i didnt know half the stuff i was eating. now gotta adjust to the time zone"

"about to start interviews here in Japan…working on

my Japanese… **おやすみなさい。** – That means "Goodnight and sweet dreams" ;-) "

"'私はあなたの電話番号を有してもいいか。'" – That is 'Can I have your phone number?' This line is very important to me while traveling this country. lol"

"got 2 start my interviews here in Tokyo…it's wild being here. Thanks 4 all the love. U guys got me traveling the world and livin a dream"

When Justin is thinking about where to go next on holiday he does a bit of research to find out what the place is like and the fun stuff that he can do there. A place might look nice but if it doesn't have a buzz around it then Justin probably wouldn't go – he wants to have lots to do when he's on holiday. He wants to go to Brazil one day because he's heard good things about it. Justin's Brazilian fans would love it if he did visit. Over three thousand fans have joined a petition on Twitter to get Justin to perform in Brazil and they have added 'Bieber in Brazil' to their profile pictures.

With tourist flights to outer space a real possibility in the next couple of years we could very well see Justin heading to other planets. It costs $20,000 to pre-book a seat with Virgin Galactic, which is a lot of money, but imagine being able to say that you'd been to space. Justin's fans would love it if he became the first singer to perform from a shuttle in outer space.

Home

Justin comes from Stratford, Ontario in Canada. He wasn't one of those kids who dreamt about becoming famous because he didn't think it was possible coming from his small town. He spelled out to *People* magazine how he used to think: "Nothing ever came out of Stratford... It's almost an impossible dream that you just don't think about."

Justin's home town is a beautiful place and was once named the prettiest city in the world. It is bursting with culture and its tourism website boasts: "We are a charming Victorian city nestled in pastoral countryside a few short hours from Toronto and the U.S. — a destination internationally renowned as one of North America's great arts towns."

Justin's take on the town was very different but that was because he was a young boy when he lived there and didn't care much for the annual Shakespeare Festival and the town's links with Stratford-upon-Avon (England) — apart from the fact that it brought the tourists who saw him busk and dropped money into his guitar case.

Justin lived with his mum when he was growing up but he also spent a lot of time at his grandpa and grandma's home. They might not have had much money but Justin never went without love. His mum's apartment was only small but it was home. She had to work so hard just to pay the rent and Justin will always be grateful for what she did to make sure that he had a roof over his head and food to eat. He must be so glad that they will never have to financially struggle ever again.

When Justin thinks back to when his mum had to work two jobs and what the apartment was like he doesn't feel like they were as poor as the press says they were. He told Macleans.ca: "I mean, some people have it misconstrued. I wasn't poor. I definitely didn't think of myself as not having a lot of money. But I definitely did not have a lot of money. I couldn't afford to get a lot of new clothes a lot of times. But I had a roof over my head. I was very fortunate. I had my grandparents, I saw them a lot, they were very kind. So I grew up getting everything that I wanted."

Once Justin signed to Def Jam Music Group he had to think long and hard about leaving Stratford and Canada behind him. He would have loved to stay at home but he needed to be where the recording studios and TV stations were – he had to make the move to Atlanta. It was 689 miles away so it was too far for him to commute!

They had to give up everything they had in Stratford and say goodbye to family and friends, but they were excited as well as being sad. They couldn't believe their dreams were about to come true.

Once in Atlanta they set about making their new place feel like home. They made new friends and explored their new city together. Atlanta is a huge city and it must have felt strange having lived in Stratford which only has a population of approximately 32,000.

Today, Justin doesn't really have a home. He travels so much that he is rarely in Atlanta and instead sleeps on a tour bus or hotel room most nights. His life is packed into a suitcase that goes with him. He's not unhappy though because his mum travels with him.

His ambition has always been to get enough money to buy his mum a house but no one knows where it will be. She might choose to have a house in Stratford, Atlanta, or maybe she would prefer a holiday home somewhere hot. Justin could buy her a couple of houses once he turns 18 and has access to the money in his trust account.

People from Justin's hometown love him so much that they have made a special map highlighting special places in Stratford where Justin used to hang out. If you want to see the map just visit www. welcometostratford.com or search in Google for 'Justin Bieber map'.

JUSTIN'S SPECIAL PLACES IN STRATFORD:

- The Avon Theatre – Where he busked
- Stratford Skate Park – Justin spent lots of time here with his mates
- William Allman Memorial Arena – Where Justin played hockey
- Kiwanis Community Centre – Where he entered the talent competition
- Jeanne Sauvé Catholic School, Stratford Northwestern Public School and Stratford Northwestern Secondary School – Justin's old schools
- The Pour House (used to be called Sid's Pub) – Justin and his mates played pool in here
- Long & McQuade Music Shop – His favourite music shop
- Cooper Standard Soccer Fields – Where Justin played football for the Stratford Strikers
- Madelyn's Diner – Pattie's favourite restaurant, they ate here a lot
- Scoopers – Justin loved eating strawberry banana yogurt cones from here after football games
- City Hall – Justin took part in a charity CD launch concert here. Check out his version of 'Set A Place at Your Table' on YouTube

• Features Restaurant – Justin liked having breakfast here

If you ever get the chance to visit Stratford you should go and see these special places. Who knows you might bump into his mates Chaz and Ryan or one of his distant relations.

Justin came from what he likes to call the smallest town in the world and he managed to become a huge star. Don't let where you come from stop you from being who you want to be.

I is for...

Inspiration

Justin has been inspired by a lot of people, even though he is only young. When he was growing up his musical heroes were Michael Jackson, Prince, Boyz II Men and Stevie Wonder. He was inspired by their talent and their musical achievements. Michael Jackson won an amazing 13 Grammys and Justin would love to follow in his footsteps.

Justin talked to *Vanity Fair* about musicians that inspire him. He said: "Music is music, and I'm definitely influenced by Michael Jackson and Boyz II Men and people who were black artists – that's what I like. But I

STEVIE WONDER IS ONE OF JUSTIN'S MANY INSPIRATIONS.

like their voices and I like how they entertain – it's not about what color they are.

"Michael (Jackson) was able to reach audiences from young to old; he never limited himself... He was so broad, everybody loved him, and that's what my goal is – to basically make people happy, to inspire them, and to have everyone root for me."

When Justin was a baby he loved it when his mum put on the radio. He enjoyed listening to music and joining in. He would sing along to Michael Jackson tracks and play his toy drum set – that his mum had given to him when he was two.

Justin loved hearing the worship band at his church play and they encouraged him to copy them. By the time he was five he was quite good and it wasn't long before he had his own proper set of drums. He was inspired by other musicians he knew, as well as the singers he heard on the radio. His family have inspired him too – especially his grandpa and his mum.

Justin was devastated when Michael Jackson died. He was so upset. He wants to try and follow Michael's example and give as much as he can back to charity. When he started to tour he decided to include a tribute to Michael.

Justin might not realise how many people he inspires every day through his music and his actions. The world would be a better place if more people were like Justin and put others before themselves.

J is for...

Jasmine Villegas

Jasmine Villegas is a talented singer and actress. She was the girl in Justin's 'Baby' video and also appeared in Kanye West's 'Jesus Walks' video and Frankie J.'s 'How To Deal' video. She had a short cameo in Justin's 'Eenie Meenie' video with Sean Kingston too. She has appeared in a few TV shows including *That's So Raven*, *My Wife and Kids* and *The Nine*.

Justin has said in interviews that he chooses the love interests in his videos from a shortlist he is given so he probably picked out Jasmine. She is stunningly beautiful and has a gorgeous personality to match.

JASMINE VILLEGAS WAS JUSTIN'S LOVE INTEREST IN THE VIDEO TO 'BABY'.

Jasmine has become a good friend of Justin's since the 'Baby' video and many people think they were boyfriend and girlfriend for a while. She is one year older than our favourite pop star and has been supporting him on tour as she was snapped up by a record company in 2010 and released her first single 'All These Boys' in October 2010.

She tried to think of something unique to say about Justin when she was being interviewed by *Bop and Tiger Beat*, but she couldn't. She admitted: "He's just so random, but I think everybody would know that.

"There's not much that I would know that people don't know because Justin is just 100 per cent [real] with his fans and his friends and he gives everybody his full personality... So that's a really good thing about him. He's not fake at all. He's just like, 'I'm Justin. Here's me.'"

Joking Around

Justin loves to joke around. He used to get in trouble at school for making people laugh in class or for being disruptive. He couldn't help it – he's just a lad who likes having fun. Sometimes when he is on stage he will tell the audience a joke before he sings. He likes the one that goes 'What do you call a fish without an eye?' 'A Fsh!'

For April Fool's Day he was being filmed by Radio

Disney and wanted to have some fun. He said he was going to sing a song from his first album but started singing 'Party in the USA' by Miley Cyrus. It was really funny.

Sometimes his pranks work and sometimes they don't. He had some joke shop chewing gum that gave people an electric shock when they tried to take a piece of gum and he managed to get a few people with that. When he was being interviewed by French radio station NRJ he tried to pull a prank on Usher by calling him up and pretending that he had broken his ankle and was on the way to hospital. Usher knows Justin really well so didn't fall for it and guessed that he was joking around.

He took things a bit too far before his performance at the Maryland State Fair. Websites reported that Justin had started throwing some water balloons with some of his crew and ended up hitting two state troopers. They didn't arrest Justin or write up an incident report because they knew that Justin was just being Justin.

Justin seems to love throwing things and when his warm-up act The Stunners were performing for the last time on tour he decided to ambush the stage and throw things at them. He was joined by a few of his mates and they had the audience screaming as the girls tried to throw things back at Justin and chase him.

Sometimes Justin gets pranked by his crew. During one performance of 'One Less Lonely Girl' they had a man in a tiara take a seat on stage as the lonely girl. Justin tried to get a real fan to take the guy's place but he picked Justin up. Afterwards Justin tweeted: "all smiles over here…great way to end the first leg of the tour..but man they got me tonight. cant help but smile and laugh. it was a good one. the prankster got pranked. anyone got video of it?"

He was also sprayed with silly string by his crew after he performed 'Baby' at the Maryland State Fair in September 2010. He might love pranking them but they love pranking him just as much.

K is for...

Kisses

Justin had his first kiss when he was 13 but he won't reveal the name of the lucky girl. He isn't very proud of the way it happened. He confessed to 958 Capital FM: "I first made out with a girl, I don't remember her name, it was at my school and it was like a school dance and basically it was kind of bad because it was my first kiss and I told my friends, I said 'First person to kiss a girl gets 10 dollars and my boys, they didn't kiss anyone and they were like 'Justin, you should do it' and I was like slow dancing with this girl and then I just went in... she just went with it I guess.

"Back then I was just like some like regular hockey-playing kid so I was lucky that she kissed me back."

In another interview with *Seventeen* magazine he said that he dated the girl he had his first kiss with for a while, so maybe he was just hiding her identity in the interview with 958 Capital FM to protect her.

Since then Justin has kissed a few girls but he hasn't found 'the one' yet. In September 2010 Justin was snapped by photographers kissing on the back seat of a car and many websites and magazines reported that Jasmine Villegas was the lucky girl. He spoke about what happened to veteran TV presenter Barbara Walters:

"I didn't even know anyone was taking pictures. It just kind of happened and I don't know. It's not really weird. Is it weird?

"I think every 16-year-old kisses a girl, right, so that's not nothing out of the ordinary… I was just kissing her. That's about it."

He answered no when she asked him if they were dating and said it was "just a kiss."

L is for...

L.A. Reid

L.A. Reid is one of the most important men in the whole of the record industry. He is the CEO of Def Jam Music Group and he was the person who signed Usher when he was a budding young singer. Usher arranged for L.A. Reid to meet Justin in April 2008 and took along Justin's mum Pattie and Scooter too.

Justin knew he had to impress L.A. Reid first and then if he did well L.A. Reid would try and get a second opinion. Usher told *Vanity Fair*: "I knew what L.A. was gonna do – the same thing he did to me. Let's bring in employees and we want to see how he reacts to women." Usher must have told Justin this so he knew what to expect.

Justin sang his heart out and gave it everything he had. He didn't find out whether he had done enough straight away, and had to go back home to Stratford and wait. When he got a phone call telling him they wanted to sign him he was over the moon. He officially signed to Def Jam Music Group on 13 April 2008.

L.A. Reid thinks that Justin is a bit like Michael Jackson, a bit like the Beatles and a bit like Elvis. Justin's fans would agree. He is so talented and will be making hit records for the rest of his life.

The music mogul told azcentral.com: "I thought he was an amazing kid, charming with loads of personality." He wasn't put off by the fact that Justin wasn't coming from a TV show, and was just a schoolboy from Stratford. "I've never had the benefit of an *American Idol* or Disney type of platform. Maybe it's dated, but we launch artists in the traditional sense. Oftentimes, while these kids may be very talented, we think of them as TV stars first, and the music is secondary. Justin is music first."

M is for...

Merchandise

If you love Justin then you might have a few pieces of Justin's merchandise. There are literally hundreds of things for sale with Justin's face on – some are official and some are unofficial.

He has released a fragrance for boys and girls called 'My World' but you can't get it in a bottle. Instead it comes in special dog tags that hold the scent for up to 12 months. The dog tags are available in a range of colours and fans are encouraged to swap and collect them with their friends. Sadly for UK fans the dog tags aren't available in the UK just yet.

It is thought that Justin will be bringing out a more traditional style perfume sometime in 2011. He talked to *People* about why it makes him different: "Most male celebrities do male colognes for other males. I think that me making a female fragrance is just a different idea and I think it's going to be successful."

Even though Justin isn't thinking about doing an aftershave just yet it is only a matter of time. Justin's fan base might be mainly female but there are still plenty of lads who like Justin's music and style.

As well as developing a fragrance line Justin has also been busy releasing some special nail varnishes for his fans. His nail-varnish range is called One Less Lonely Girl collection for Nicole by OPI and came out in the USA just before Christmas. Fans can choose from Prized Possession Purple (dark purple) One Less Lonely Glitter (lavender), My Lifesaver (mint green), Me + Blue (dark blue), Me The First Dance (silver), Step 2 the Beat of My Heart (clear with metallic stars and glitter) and OMB! (red). All of Justin's nail varnishes are really glittery and fans have been raving about them because they look so good and don't streak as much as some nail varnishes do. In buying a bottle they are also helping the Pencils of Promise charity because OPI agreed with Justin that some of the profits would go to his favourite charity. It's not known if the nail-varnish line will be released in the UK.

If you visit his official website www.justinbieber.com you can purchase mugs, hoodies, t-shirts, vests, pyjamas, phone covers, bracelets, notepads, gift tags, his book, his calendar and even Justin Bieber pillows.

Money

Justin might have millions in the bank but he can't touch a penny of it until his 18th birthday. He only gets £30 ($50) in pocket money a day and if he wants something he has to save up like any normal teenager. Scooter thinks it's important that the majority of Justin's money goes into the trust fund because it helps Justin stay focused. He explained to journalist Liz Jones what happens if child stars are given control of their money straight away: "The child becomes the breadwinner and the parents don't know how to deal with them. They are terrified of upsetting the kid."

Justin doesn't seem to mind that he can't access his money just yet and knows that his mum is teaching him how to 'be smart' with money. You will never see him throwing it away on silly things because he believes his wealth is a gift from God and he wants to use it to help as many people as he can.

Justin's success has also earned his record company, Usher and Scooter a lot of money but during the same interview Scooter announced: "I'm a smart guy. I would be wealthy without Justin Bieber."

DID YOU KNOW?

Justin spends his allowance using a credit card rather than carrying cash. He doesn't even have a wallet yet.

Movies

Justin was so excited when he told his fans that he was bringing out his own movie for the first time.

He announced that *Never Say Never 3D* would be released in Spring 2011 and it would be a documentary style movie. The director was Jon Chu who had previously directed *Step Up 3D* and *Step Up 2: The Streets*. Jon explained to *USA Today* why they decided to call the movie *Never Say Never*: "It's from one of his songs, but also the idea of every moment in his life. When he was a kid, some people said, 'You can't play the drums,' and he did. Or, 'You can post it on the Internet, but no one will see it.' Then millions of people saw it."

Justin's fans couldn't wait to see the movie and they

NEVER SAY NEVER 3D DIRECTOR JON CHU.

were glad in some ways that only about 20 per cent of *Never Say Never 3D* was about Justin performing on stage. The vast majority of fans were more interested in seeing Justin behind the scenes and hearing what life was like for him before he got famous. They were also looking forward to seeing more home movie clips of when Justin was a toddler.

In the run-up to the movie being released Justin kept tweeting about it. On 4th January he tweeted: "everyday people ask me about different rumors. well I guess my new answer will be wait until #NEVERSAYNEVER3D. it answers them all

"what is the goal of #NEVERSAYNEVER3D? I guess to tell the story about hope and try to inspire other kids to go after their dreams....

"it's not even just about me. from @scooterbraun to @studiomama to @thatrygood and @kenny hamilton and even my fans...we are all underdogs but we believed in each other. that is what #NEVERSAYNEVER3D is really about. Less than 6weeks away and super proud of it. cant wait 2 share."

The movie was such a big hit around the world when it was released in February. Many fans saw it more than once and their big wish is that Justin does another movie soon. They loved getting their limited edition purple 3D glasses and can't wait for the movie to be released on DVD.

JUSTIN'S FAVOURITE MOVIES:

- *The Notebook* starring Ryan Gosling and Rachel McAdams. This is Justin's favourite girly movie.

- *Rocky IV* starring Sylvester Stallone. This movie came out in 1985 but Justin, like other fans of the Rocky series, thinks it's a classic.

- *A Walk to Remember* starring Mandy Moore. This is another girly movie based on a book

THE NOTEBOOK STARS, RYAN GOSLING AND RACHEL McADAMS.

by the same author as *The Notebook* – Nicholas Sparks.

- *Cars* by Disney Pixar. Justin's favourite cartoon movie.
- *Step Up* starring Channing Tatum. This is a dance-drama movie.
- *Drumline* starring Nick Cannon. This movie is a music-drama movie.

- *You Got Served* starring boy band B2K. It was released in 2004 and is another dance-drama.
- *Saving Private Ryan* starring Matt Damon and Tom Hanks. This is a moving war movie.

ROCKY IV STAR, SYLVESTER STALLONE.

When you take a look at Justin's favourite movies you can see he is very fond of movies that have a strong dance and music storyline, and some romance. His movie list contains movies he would watch with his mum, his mates, his crew and even his little brother and sister (*Cars!*).

His favourite movie of all time must be *Never Say Never 3D* because it is his movie and tells his life story. He has watched it so many times already but he will never tire of it.

Mum

Justin's mum is called Pattie Mallette and she was 18 years old when he was born. Justin's mum went back to her maiden name after her divorce from Justin's dad Jeremy. Pattie is a Christian and brought Justin up in the church – so he learnt about God and Jesus from a very early age.

When Justin misbehaves his mum isn't afraid to ground him. She will take his computer or his phone. Justin thinks she's quite strict. They are really close and only argue about small things, about places he wants to go and other trivial stuff. They probably wouldn't argue with each other if they didn't spend so much time together every single day.

She thinks he is growing up too fast, but at the same time thinks that every mum feels the same way.

Justin's mum had a hard time when she was growing up and she was abused from when she was five until she was about ten. Her biological dad left when she was three and her sister died, so poor Pattie really had a rough time coping with things. She kept all the hurt inside and didn't tell anyone. When she became a teenager she started to drink and take drugs so she could forget about all the bad things. She would go to school drunk and when she turned 15 she decided to leave home and moved in with four guys.

She admitted to the presenter of *The Full Circle* that by the time she was 17 she wanted to die so she decided to walk in front of a truck. She just wanted it to be all over. Thankfully the driver managed to slam on his brakes and turned into a side road. Pattie ended up on a mental ward because she had tried to kill herself. She revealed: "I didn't have any 'friends' come visit me, I realised I didn't really have any friends at that point but I used to hang out at a youth centre and the director of the youth centre was a Christian man... and he ended up coming to visit me in the hospital and he brought a rose." Pattie accepted the rose and thought it was pretty insignificant because, after all, people buy flowers for sick people in hospital all the time. What he said to her changed her opinion on the rose and on life. Pattie recalls: "He said 'I want you to know that God told me to bring this to you and he wants me to tell you that he sees you like this rose.' And I was thinking, 'Oh my gosh this man obviously doesn't hear from God, if God's even real because I am not a rose, I am like living in sin... I'm stealing, I'm sleeping around, I'm doing drugs and alcohol, I'm not a rose to God.'"

Pattie let him keep visiting her because he brought her fast food, she wasn't interested at first but she decided one day to give God a chance. She prayed and invited Jesus into her life and she hasn't looked back since. As she prayed she had a vision of a picture of her heart being opened and "tons and tons of sparkle dust, so much so much, pour into my heart and I... just knew that it was love."

Justin knows bits about his mum's past and told a reporter from *The Guardian*:

"My mom wasn't the greatest person. I mean, she was a good person, but she made mistakes. She drank. She probably did drugs and stuff, and she told me about it because she said she did enough bad stuff for the both of us."

It's scary to think that Justin would never have been born if that truck had hit Pattie. She has completely turned her life around.

When Justin was asked by the backstage interviewer on *The Oprah Show* what he loves about his mum the most he replied: "I love that she's just a really strong woman, she's been there since day one and just wanted me to be the best person that I can possibly be. She doesn't care about the money, the fame, she just wants to be my mom."

Pattie is constantly telling people how proud she is of Justin on twitter. Here are some of her best tweets: "Luv u justin ur the best son ever.. I'm glad ur so well behaved ur such an angel."

"Ok so my phone died before I could finish my tweets! Congrats baby boy! You deserve the best & to God be all the glory!! 'Pray' was AMAZING!"

"I just saw a screening of the best movie ever! #neversaynever So proud! & no. Its NOT a concert movie. Its an inspiring life story thus far!"

If you want to follow Pattie you can, her twitter address is http://twitter.com/studiomama. Pattie tweets about Justin, what they are up to and inspirational verses from the Bible.

Music

Justin taught himself how to play the piano, guitar and drums, which took real dedication. His mum could have never afforded to pay for lessons because she had to work several jobs just to pay the rent and buy food.

Justin was two when he started playing the drums and he was five when he started playing the piano. He couldn't read music but by practising again and again he taught himself how to play in tune. Justin loved playing the toy drum set his mum had bought him but he outgrew it and needed a bigger set. His mum's friends at church and their neighbours knew Justin was talented and began fund-raising so that Justin could have a really great drum kit. They held a special fundraiser called 'The Justin Bieber Benefit Concert' and several local bands and singers performed. The

flyer for the event stated: "At 8 years old Justin Bieber's talent as a drummer can only be described as exceptional.

"That is why the 'Building Dreams Team' has come together with yet another drum kit benefit. All proceeds from this benefit will go directly to the purchase of a drum kit for Justin with thanks to Stratford's businesses, musicians, and volunteers for the evening's production.

"COME $HOW YOUR $UPPORT!!!

"TOGETHER WE CAN MAKE THIS HAPPEN."

Justin performed with a band called Miles Beyond and the audience loved it. They cheered and clapped for Justin who was just eight years old at the time. His whole family were so grateful for everyone who had paid $5 to go to the concert and for everyone who helped get Justin his drum kit. Footage of Justin playing can be seen on his official YouTube channel (just search for kidrauhl).

In the same year Justin started learning how to play the guitar and after a bit of practice he became pretty good.

He told ABC News: "Basically when I started playing the guitar, I picked up a right-handed guitar. 'Cause that was all … my mom had a right-handed guitar in the house. And picked it up and I picked it up left-handed.

My mom would switch it the other way. And I would switch it right back to the other way and try to play. It was difficult because it's backwards. My mom, I think it was for my birthday, she bought me a left-handed guitar. And so ever since I was young I learned on a left-handed guitar."

His dad helped him quite a bit too because he is a talented guitarist. Justin also plays the trumpet.

Justin confided to MTV: "People at school didn't even know I could sing, but I played sport and people were jealous – always calling me a show-off. But I tried not to take it too seriously."

The kids in his class must have been so shocked when he announced he was moving to Atlanta and had secured a record deal. They must be kicking themselves now, wishing they had been nicer to Justin. If they had they might be going to celebrity events with Justin, Chaz and Ryan.

DID YOU KNOW?

No one in Justin's family had ever had a music career or performed professionally but they are all quite musical. His grandma is an accomplished pianist, writes her own songs and sings too. His dad plays the guitar and sings, and his mum sings as well. Obviously they aren't in the same league as Justin when it comes to singing.

In one of the first videos Justin uploaded on YouTube he sang a song his grandma had written.

N is for...

Nick Jonas

Many people see Nick Jonas as one of Justin's biggest rivals. They are both hugely successful recording artists, Christians, and share many of the same friends. Justin's friend Miley Cyrus used to date Nick when she was younger and she gets on with both Nick and Justin.

What caused people to say that Nick and Justin are enemies was that fans of Justin and fans of the Jonas Brothers were fighting it out in internet forums. One fan would ask 'Who is better Justin or Nick?' and then fans from both camps would come up with huge lists of

NICK JONAS, JUSTIN'S BIGGEST RIVAL.

why their favourite singer was the best and why the other person was rubbish.

In one interview Nick and his brothers admitted that they call Justin 'Bustin Jieber'. Justin's fans weren't very happy and only a few days later Justin and Nick ended up at the White House together. They had both been invited to the Correspondents Dinner. Rather than ignore each other they decided to have a chat and left with plans to meet up again. Justin told his fans via twitter: "also @nickjonas and i talked about the Bustin Jieber thing. all good. great guy. Lookin forward to playing Jick Nonas in ping pong soon. lol"

And Nick wrote in response, "@justinbieber Haha dude... Maybe George Glooney will want to play ping pong too. Good seeing you tonight bro."

He also started following Justin on twitter which shows that Nick wanted to get to know Justin more. Fans of both stars decided to let bygones be bygones and soon Kick Nonas became a trending topic on twitter – as fans of both Nick and Justin started retweeting Justin's message.

O is for...

Oprah

The day Justin was interviewed by Oprah was so, so special. Justin, his mum and his whole family were so thrilled that the biggest chat-show host in the world wanted to have Justin on her show. Oprah only has the best of the best on her programme and many stars would do anything to get a spot on her couch.

Justin took part in an episode of her chat show called *World's Most Talented Kids*. Oprah asked him about his journey from being a schoolboy to being a big star, how he handles fame, what had been the most exciting thing that had happened to him and how he

CHAT-SHOW HOST, OPRAH WINFREY.

feels about his fans. Justin also got to make three fans' dreams come true on the show, which was very touching. The Simons sisters had been planning on going to see Justin in concert with their dad but then he got deployed to Iraq. Oprah and Justin decided to make it up to the girls by giving them front-row seats and letting them ride in a limo with Justin. Oprah managed to get their dad to appear on Skype from Iraq, and he said to Justin: "Oprah, you just made me father of the year for the next decade." Justin then told their dad: "When you get back, we're going to have five tickets waiting for you and your family to come to my concert on my tour."

Once Justin left the set he let the fact that he had just been on the *Oprah Show* sink in and then tweeted: "Just got to say that Oprah is real nice down to earth person. She even came back after the show to talk with everyone. She is incredible. And she made my grandpa cry. He went all water works in the crowd."

He went on Facebook too and told his fans on there: "Couldn't believe she was interviewing me. It was surreal. Thanks to everyone who worked hard to get me there. Really an honor and a testament to the incredible fans that you all are. Thank you. Really."

His mum felt like adding her own message and tweeted: "So proud!!! My son just did Oprah!

@justinbieber was so charming! It airs May 11th! I was on for a minute too!! So exciting!"

If you didn't see Justin on Oprah then you should visit her official website to find out what he said and watch a fab backstage interview. Her website address is simply www.oprah.com.

Oscars

Justin might be more of a singer than an actor but that didn't stop him getting shortlisted for an Oscar!

Some actors go their whole lives without being shortlisted but Justin managed it when he was just 16. It seems like it wasn't just Justin's fans who loved *Never Say Never* as it made the cut for the Original Song category.

Many people think that the 2012 Oscars will see Justin nominated for a lot more Oscars as his movie *Never Say Never 3D* will be eligible. It would be great if he won an Oscar or two because it would shut his haters up once and for all.

When the *Bop and Tiger Beat* website asked whether Justin should win an Oscar and a Grammy in 2011 his fans quickly replied to say "Yes!"

Super fan Biebersigns wrote: "Um…Are You Insane! OF COURSE He Should Get Them Both, The Kid Is Drop Dead Talented. He Earns It All!"

Bieber472 added: "I hope justin wins cuz he's earned it and deserves it. He always makes sure his music makes his fans happy and that's why he is a great artist. I love him and know he will win. Love ya Justin. Always will. Xoxoxo."

P is for...

President Obama

President Obama is the most powerful man in the world and Justin has met him twice already.

The first time Justin met President Obama was on Sunday 13 December 2009 when he was invited to take part in the *Christmas in Washington* special with Usher. It's a special Christmas TV programme in the USA and raises money for a charity chosen by Michelle Obama, the National Children's Medical Center.

He tweeted: "in DC preparing to sing for President OBAMA!! yeah im nervous. if i mess up he might deport me back to Canada. lol"

JUSTIN IS LUCKY ENOUGH TO HAVE MET PRESIDENT OBAMA TWICE!

He had an amazing time and posted a photo on twitter of himself with Usher, the President and his wife Michelle. Sadly whoever took the photo didn't hold the camera steady so it is quite fuzzy.

A few days later he posted up the video on his YouTube channel and wrote this special message underneath: "These past 2 years have been amazing...I have gone from singing in my little town of Stratford to singing the same song, SOMEDAY AT CHRISTMAS by Stevie Wonder, to the President of the United States! It was an incredible honor and I was really nervous. You can tell by my hands, I didn't know what to do with them. I was like Will Ferrell in Talladega Nights. haha. But what I am getting at is that all this has happened thanks to YouTube videos and fans like you. You have all changed my life forever."

The next time Justin met the Obamas was on 5 April 2010. It is not very often that President Obama is made to look foolish but when it came to introducing Justin at the annual Easter Egg Roll he made a big mistake. He pronounced Justin's surname as 'BYE-ber' and not 'BEE-ber.'

Justin didn't really mind and told *People* magazine: "He messed up my name, but I give it to him. He's not (the) age category I sing to. He's not 'One Less Lonely Girl'."

JUSTIN HAS ALSO MET FORMER PRESIDENT, BILL CLINTON.

Justin was just happy to be there and to be asked to perform to the 30,000 people in the audience. He kept tweeting his fans all day:

"they had snipers and secret service around but the President let 30k people onto the lawn. pretty cool…

"I got to go into the White House and get a tour and a pic with the first family. they are really nice and had a lot of fun but after 3 performances in 90 degree hot sun…Im completely dehydrated and almost passed out after the last one….need to drink some water.

"thanks to everyone who came out today…it was a pretty incredible experience and I am grateful for the honor. Thanks to all the fans."

Justin will no doubt be invited to future Easter Egg Rolls because he was such a big hit. He will treasure every moment he has spent with the President and his family, especially the time he spent in the Oval Office. Not many people are allowed in that special room so Justin felt really blessed to chat to the President in there.

Protection

Kenny Hamilton is in charge of protecting Justin. He is a super bodyguard and Justin knows he is safe hands when he is there by his side. Justin is the first person Kenny has looked after because he used to be a DJ before

Scooter gave him the job of being in charge of Justin's security. Kenny was a friend of Scooter's and just started helping out when Justin wanted to go places – then the job came up and he was the perfect person to do it.

Kenny has become famous just for being Justin's bodyguard. He has more than 170,000 followers on Twitter and his account had to be verified because people were pretending to be him. He says in his Twitter description: "Hard working making people smile…"

Kenny will do whatever it takes to protect Justin and if he had to take a bullet for him he would. His job is to hold back the paparazzi when they try to ambush Justin and make sure that Justin can move around safely. He doesn't protect Justin on his own now because Justin can have hundreds of people following him at one time but in the beginning when Justin was just starting out he travelled on his own with Justin's mum. Kenny is in charge of a whole team of people who protect Justin because it is a 24-hour, 7-days-a-week job.

In the past, when Justin wouldn't listen to something Pattie was telling him, then she has asked Kenny to intervene. Justin listens to Kenny and really values him as a good friend, not just his bodyguard. Scooter, his girlfriend, Kenny and the rest of Justin's backstage team are like family to Justin and he couldn't imagine his life without them.

Some of Justin's haters have made horrible comments in the past about Kenny being on the large side in their blogs, but according to journalist Sandra Rose this inspired him to lose 40 pounds. Kenny does look a lot fitter than he did but most grown men would look big next to Justin because he is so slim.

Kenny is fair with Justin's fans and he will let them see Justin if it is safe and time allows it. If Justin is in a rush and needs to be somewhere then Kenny will try and get him out of a building and into the car in the fastest time possible. Kenny, like all bodyguards, is always looking out for dangers and has an escape route planned out. If fans try to give him things to pass on to Justin then he can't take them because he needs to concentrate on Justin's safety. If you have a letter or gift to pass on to Justin then the best thing to do is to send it to his fan mail address.

Q is for...

Questions

Justin has done thousands of interviews all around the world and sometimes gets asked the same questions by journalists. The best interviews are the ones where his fans set the questions.

When Radio Disney asked fans to submit questions for their interview with Justin they received 1,500 questions and 4,000 fans voted for their favourite three. This proves how popular Justin is.

One of the questions fans wanted to know the answer to was 'How does it feel to be a celebrity and do you have any advice for someone wanting to make it

big?' Justin replied: "My advice is that hard work pays off, as well as following your dreams and always putting God first is something, you know, you have to realise.

"I never knew what went on behind the scenes (before getting a record deal). I was just Justin. I didn't know there were photo shoots, I didn't know there was a lot of press you had to do but you know something you have to do alongside what you do... I just try to have fun with it you know."

Sometimes Justin gets asked questions he doesn't like and isn't prepared to answer. *Heat* magazine asked him during one interview whether he had a girlfriend. He said: "I think that question is just asked way too much. I'm not going to be able to have a personal life if I keep being asked that question. So I'm not answering that question ever again." Fans might like to find out about Justin's love life but in many ways it is better that Justin has banned this question from interviews because too often journalists are more interested in girls he might be dating than his actual music. Some extreme fans will send girls they think Justin is seeing hate mail and death threats – scary stuff!

To run alongside an interview Justin might have a photo shoot with a magazine or his people might just supply the magazine with a photo of Justin they have already taken. Magazines usually choose a nice photo for the magazine but sometimes Justin and his fans aren't happy with the way Justin is portrayed.

Fans hated the cover of Brazilian Magazine, *Todateen Star*, and thought that lipstick and eyeshadow had been added in postproduction. They started tweeting about it and in the end the magazine decided to defend itself by releasing a statement to the *Huffington Post*. Their response was originally in Portuguese but translated it reads:

"We could not help noticing your comments and tweets from the picture of Justin on the magazine's cover. We would like to say there was no change made in the area of the singer's eyes. We had a technical problem that darkens certain areas of the photo.

"We also want to say that all of us find Justin very naturally beautiful. We'd never think it necessary to alter pictures of him. Natural beauty says it all, right?"

Justin didn't comment on the matter himself, but he did express his dislike of the front cover of *People* magazine, a hugely popular USA publication. In the photo he is laughing and many fans would say it doesn't really look like the Justin we know and love. He tweeted: "Dear @peoplemag Covershoot…next time i laugh real crazy warn me u r still taking pics…still appreciate u but let's get on the same page."

The message didn't stay up for long and was quickly

replaced with: "EXCLUSIVE story and pics in the new issue of @peoplemag . I look crazy as heck on the cover but if u cant laugh at yourself u aint havin fun."

R is for...

Rest

Everyone needs time to rest but when you're the biggest pop star on the planet it can be really hard.

Justin told Oprah: "We try to take off at least one day a week for me to be a regular kid, go play basketball, hang out with my friends and, you know, just do what I like to do. Sometimes for that day I just sleep all day because the six days before I'm exhausted."

When *Seventeen* magazine asked Justin about the last dream he had, he said: "I dreamt about blackness because I don't dream. I just fall asleep, see black, and wake up."

People think that being a celebrity is easy but it isn't. Justin has to work long hours as he does school work as well as his music stuff. When he was on tour people thought he would have plenty of time off in the day but he had interviews to do and had to travel from venue to venue.

Travelling far from home takes its toll on Justin as he explained to *The Guardian*: "You're so far away, and you start feeling like you're a robot. When I'm overseas the schedule is always crazy and then there's the time change and you're not even yourself. It's weird."

Justin also likes to visit his little brother and sister in Canada when he can so that means hectic days as he tries to catch up with them. Justin wouldn't change his job for anything though because he feels so blessed. He knows there are millions of people who would like to be in his shoes right now.

Sometimes when Justin does have a week or so off he doesn't rest because he finds it boring. He likes doing fun activities with his mates instead. When he gets sick he has no choice and has to have a few days resting so he can get better. Even when he feels okay he might have to rest his voice so won't do as many interviews as usual. Performing every night on stage can be tiring and sometimes Justin's throat just needs a rest.

> ### DID YOU KNOW?
>
> Justin is so busy that he hardly gets chance to watch TV. He does like *Smallville* and *Grey's Anatomy* but he's usually performing when they're on. It must be so nice when he can chill out, put his feet up and catch up on all the TV that he's missed.

Rumours

Every celebrity in the world hates the fact that people love spreading rumours about them. The rumours hurt them, their families, their friends and their fans. Sometimes fans can mistakenly think a rumour is true and start to worry unnecessarily.

Gossip websites and blogs have said that Justin has died about five times now which is really frustrating for Justin and his family. Justin can't always pre-warn the people he is closest to when there is going to be one of these death stories and imagine what it must be like for them to turn on their computers and read that Justin has been in a car accident. Some Justin haters even make authentic looking YouTube videos which make it seem like news reporters are at the crash scene and are reporting on Justin's death. It really is shocking how people can get pleasure out of upsetting Justin and his fans in this way.

In the first six months of 2010 alone there were three rumours circulated that Justin had died. The first time was on 5 January, the second time was on 22 February and the third time was on 10 June.

On one of these occasions Justin tweeted as soon as he could to let his fans know he was safe. He said: "and another rumor that I died?? The craziest stuff happens when I get on long plane rides. lol. Im ALIVE and well and very blessed. thanks."

Sometimes rumours are spread that accuse Justin of being moody and rude. It was reported that in April 2010 when Justin was in Australia he swore at a TV producer and warned him off touching him again. Justin defended himself when he tweeted: "Gonna take some time to chill and spend some quality family time with @studiomama (his mum)

"Family time with my mom couldn't come at a better time….i was raised to respect others and not gossip…nor answer gossip with anger.

"I know my friends family and fans know the person i am. hearing adults spread lies and rumors is part of the job i guess.

"But i all i have to say is…kill em with kindness. So everyone keep smiling…we r all blessed and I am still grateful and appreciate of the opportunity u have all given me to do what i love."

Justin handled the whole situation really well and didn't decide to retaliate or hurl insults at the TV producer or the media outlets that reported the story. He proved once again that he won't let bullies get him down.

There will always be rumours about Justin circulating in the press and on the web because stories on Justin sell magazines and get people clicking on certain websites. Justin will have to keep putting the record straight for his fans so they know what the truth is.

S is for...

School

Justin started out at Jeanne Sauvé Catholic School in Stratford. It is a French immersion school which meant that Justin and his friends had to have all their lessons in French. Their teachers didn't speak English to them so they had to quickly pick up French so they could learn everything else.

Justin moved from Jeanne Sauvé Catholic School after his elementary grades to Stratford Northwestern Public School for grades seven and eight.

In this school Justin was known for playing hockey and he found his best friends Chaz Somers and Ryan

JUSTIN REALLY
ENJOYED HOCKEY
AND SKATEBOARDING
WHILST HE WAS AT
SCHOOL.

Butler through the game. They all loved hockey and wanted to be great players. Justin's favourite teachers at school were Miss Booker and Mr Monteith. He didn't really like going to lessons and preferred being on the sports field. If he had to pick a lesson he disliked the least then he would probably pick English. He hated maths the most.

Mr Monteith remembers Justin well and thinks he was fearless and very gifted at picking up new things. There wasn't anything that Justin couldn't excel in if he put his mind to it. When he was still at school he was great at any sports he tried as well as music, dance… even singing. Miss Booker has told people she thought Justin was a good singer from grade seven – but Justin never mentions singing at school in any interviews he gives and says that he kept his singing and musical talent hidden from his classmates. Singing and music was something he mainly did at home until he entered the talent competition when he was 12.

Justin was so mischievous at school that he thought he could trick his mum into thinking he had got a B in an exam by using his teacher's pen to change his F grade to a B. His mum had to sign a form to say that she had seen Justin's mark, and she did so willingly, thinking that Justin had done well.

Justin didn't just lie on that occasion, as he revealed

to *Top of the Pops* magazine: "It's not the first time I've lied. I told her I'd baked her a cake for her birthday once, but I really just bought it from a baker. I would've if I knew how, but I was afraid I'd mess it up."

Justin has changed a lot since then and always tries to be honest with his mum, his family, his friends and his fans. He would never lie to his fans; he loves them all too much.

The last school that Justin went to in Stratford was called Stratford Northwestern Secondary School and he stayed here until he moved to Atlanta. Ryan and Chaz are still there.

Once in Atlanta Justin started recording and promoting his music but he still had to fit in school. He might have been really busy but he was far too young to legally leave school and so a private tutor had to be found. Jenny, a teacher from the School of Young Performers, was given the job of tutoring Justin. Lots of young singers have tutors from the same school – Miley Cyrus and Rihanna are just two of the famous pupils. Jenny and the other tutors don't treat their pupils any differently than normal high-school kids. They can be quite strict and don't let them get away with not handing homework in on time.

Justin told reporters at the Madrid press conference for *My Worlds: The Collection*: "I always travel with a private tutor who I have five three-hour sessions a week with. I want to finish high school and also university and then evolve wherever my music takes me.

"I also want to stick my head in the movie world, although I am going to focus on my music for now."

Justin has never revealed Jenny's surname in the press so she can walk about without fans following her and asking for her to pass gifts on to Justin. They have a professional relationship but Justin can still talk to her like a friend. Sometimes she sets Justin really hard homework and he has asked fans for help before.

On 15th July he tweeted a photo of himself sitting doing homework and the caption underneath read: "Quick break. trying 2 figure out if my new angle on life is acute or obtuse. When am I actually gonna use this stuff?"

When Justin was interviewed by *The Guardian* they asked what it is like to be home-schooled (or away-schooled as Justin likes to call it.) He said: "I only have to do three hours a day, which is good. I drift off. I definitely drift off. So I'm better one-on-one. I'm way too hard on myself. I always want to be better."

The journalist went on to ask if Justin had ADD (Attention Deficit Disorder). He replied: "I have a small case of ADD... If I don't understand something, and I'm bored, I don't pay attention so my teacher has to really make it fun for me." Justin has a short break every hour and then goes back to studying. This helps improve his concentration and stops him drifting off.

Justin has never been diagnosed with ADD by a doctor, he just thinks he might have it.

DID YOU KNOW?

Justin is very bright and has a 4.0 grade point average which is the equivalent to an A grade in the UK. In the USA you usually need a 3.0 grade point average to get into university. Having his own private tutor must have helped Justin achieve this grade.

Once Justin finishes studying Jenny will probably leave his team and go on to teach another young star starting out.

Scooter Braun

Scooter is Justin's manager and along with his girlfriend Carin has become like family to Justin and his mum over the last two years. They couldn't imagine their lives without each other now but in the beginning Pattie was very wary of Scooter because she wanted to make sure that the right man was managing her son.

Here is the story of how Scooter found Justin…

Justin and his mum had no idea that uploading videos of Justin singing in a talent show competition to YouTube would result in Justin getting a record deal and becoming the biggest star on the planet. Pattie just wanted friends and family who couldn't be there to be able to see how talented Justin was and how well he performed in the show.

The day Scooter saw one of Justin's videos for the first time he hadn't been endlessly searching YouTube for videos of talented kids like many people think. He explained to azcentral.com: "I was consulting for an act that Akon had in a production deal and looking at his YouTube videos. The kid was singing Aretha Franklin's 'Respect'. and there was a related video of Justin singing the same song. I clicked on it thinking it was the same kid and realized that the 20-year-old I was watching was now 12."

Scooter wasn't the first person in the music business to see Justin's videos, many tried and failed to get him. Justin explained what made Scooter different from the rest to Macleans.ca: "I was contacted by many different record executives, a lot of different managers and agents. My mom was basically like, 'Justin, I don't think this is going to happen, it's not going to work, we don't have a lawyer, we don't have money for a lawyer, and we're not going to just sign something that we don't know what it says.' So we ended up just declining all these people.

"And this one guy, his name's Scooter, he was trying to contact my family. He got in contact with my school board, with my great-aunt that I've never met before, and ended up getting in contact with my aunt, who passed the message to my mom. And my mom was like, 'Who is this guy?' And then she went and called him to get rid of him. They ended up having a two-hour conversation. My mom had that gut feeling. I think moms generally know when they have their gut feelings. This guy offered to fly us to Atlanta no strings attached. That was basically how it started."

Justin's mum prayed a lot before they made the trip because she wanted to make sure that she was doing the right thing. She had always thought that Justin would be mentored by a Christian and be signed to a Christian label – but Scooter was Jewish. She prayed long and hard with people from her church and on her own too.

Once Justin and Pattie met with Scooter in Atlanta they realised how genuine he was and set about doing exactly what he wanted them to do. Scooter explained to the *New York Times*: "I wanted to build him up more on YouTube first," he said. "We supplied more content. I said: 'Justin, sing like there's no one in

the room. But let's not use expensive cameras.' We'll give it to kids, let them do the work, so that they feel like it's theirs."

Scooter then got Justin to record some demos and he tried to get people to listen to the tracks and take a chance on Justin. He didn't let Justin stop making his YouTube videos though. Justin might not have had Disney or Nickelodeon behind him but he had plenty of talent. Scooter was determined that they would succeed. He got people talking about Justin and once Usher saw Justin's videos on YouTube he knew he wanted to meet him.

In the end both Usher and Justin Timberlake wanted to sign Justin so Scooter let Justin meet them both and then they decided who would be the best mentor for Justin. Justin had actually met Usher in a car park the day he met Scooter for the first time but Usher brushed him off.

Journalist Nicholas Kohler asked Justin what happened with Usher and Justin Timberlake and he spilled: "I was going to a studio in Atlanta to meet some people and Usher was there, he was rolling up at the same time. It was kind of weird, I'd never seen a famous person before. So I ran up to him. I was like, 'Usher, Usher, I love your songs, can I sing you one?' And he said no in the politest possible way. Like, 'Well, let's just

JUSTIN POSES FOR A PHOTO WITH KIM KARDASHIAN.

go inside, little buddy, it's cold out.' So I didn't end up getting to sing for him. I was a little bit disappointed. Back in Canada I told everybody, 'Yeah, I met Usher,' and they were like, 'Yeah, right.'

"I got a call a week later from Scooter who said Usher saw my videos and was like, 'This kid's very talented,' and offered to fly me back to Atlanta again. So we were like, 'Why not?' We flew back to Atlanta, had a meeting with Usher, it went great. He wanted to sign me right then and there. But we'd already scheduled a meeting with Justin Timberlake. Justin and Usher are definitely rivals in the industry. They both wanted to sign me and we basically ended up going with Usher. They were both great guys, but it came down to my lawyers making the final decision."

Because Justin's lawyers went with the deal offered by Usher, Scooter was given a much bigger say than he would have if Justin had gone to Justin Timberlake.

He revealed to azcentral.com: "Usher didn't have a label yet, so he wanted to be my partner. Timberlake wanted to be my partner, but the people running his label weren't as keen on it. Usher understood the role I wanted him to play."

Justin ended up signing a multi-rights deal with Raymond Braun Music Group, which was the name Usher and Scooter picked for their new partnership.

They then signed a 50/50 joint venture with L.A. Reid's Island Def Jam Music Group in July 2008.

Scooter is Justin's friend but sometimes he has to tell Justin off. He talked to Liz Jones from *You* magazine about how their relationship works. He said: "He is the son I didn't have. If he has done something wrong, he has to apologise. Justin isn't treated with kid gloves. I've sacked people who have pandered to him. He's a kid. He's not perfect. You have to set boundaries, consistencies."

Justin is determined to be a recording artist for a very long time and Scooter wants to be there with him, every step of the way. He admitted to *The Hollywood Reporter* that Justin is determined to learn from other people's mistakes: "Justin doesn't study the people who made it... he studies the people who haven't. He hears all the naysayers about how he's going to disappear, so he likes to look up people who used to be the so-called Justin Biebers before him and didn't go anywhere. He wants to see why they didn't go anywhere. The general feeling we get is that it had nothing to do with their talent and everything to do with their personal life. Like the kids fall into drugs and destroy their own trajectory."

There is no way Pattie would let him take drugs because she knows how drugs can ruin your life. Justin

Selena Gomez, one of Justin's closest friends.

wouldn't want to anyway, he's too focused on what he wants to achieve. He would never want to let God, his family or his fans down by taking drugs.

Selena Gomez

Selena Gomez is a very talented actress and singer from Texas. She is best known for playing Alex Russo in the Disney TV show *Wizards of Waverley Place*. She is one of Justin's closest friends and many of his fans believe that they have dated in the past or are still dating now. No one is 100 per cent sure.

The dating rumours started in early December when they were spotted having pancakes together at Philadelphia's International House of Pancakes. The website TMZ suggested that they had been cuddling and holding hands but Selena denied anything was going on when she was interviewed by MTV a few days later. She said: "It was pancakes! Oh my gosh! (Justin) is one of my best friends… it was just pancakes!

"Who doesn't like pancakes? We were both performing in the same place so we went and had pancakes together. That's all it is. All innocent."

Selena has said in the past that she wouldn't date Justin because it "would be too weird." She is two years older than Justin and that makes her feel like his big sister.

Fans suspected something might have been going on because their families spent Thanksgiving together. She also talks about how cute he is in interviews. "He's a dork, he really is," she told BBC Switch, "He's so sweet. Every time we hang out I love it because the Bieber comes off, it's just like chill and it's very fun and you see that he's a 16-year-old kid who's really enjoying what he does."

She has also said in the past during a radio interview with Kidd Kraddick: "He's the cutest, sweetest kid on the face of this planet. I feel like a cougar because I totally have a crush on him."

When photos of the two of them kissing on holiday appeared online in the first week of January lots of Justin's fans were upset. Some people took it too far though by tweeting that they would kill Selena if she was dating Justin.

DID YOU KNOW?

Justin sometimes feels small when he's standing next to Selena. She confessed to *Sugar* magazine: "Last time I wore high heels next to him, he asked me to take them off because he didn't want to be shorter than me. I was laughing and going 'No, I'm not going to take them off, you're not going to make me take my shoes off!'"

Songs

Justin has always listened to songs from different genres and thinks it's good to have a broad taste in music. When he was growing up he liked the song 'God Is Bigger Than the Boogie Man' from the Christian cartoon series *Veggie Tales* and Boyz II Men's classic 'On Bended Knee'.

Now he is writing and recording his own music Justin feels like he should try to mix it up a bit. He confided in *Details* magazine: "I just think that if you're a musical artist you should do something that appeals to all ages. I mean, I have songs that are about love, but I have songs that are about everyday life and stuff that people can relate to. When I was very young my parents split up, and that was hard on me. So I have a song that talks about that. I want to have a career, not just a hit."

Justin loves making the videos for his singles because he gets a good looking love interest to sing to and there are other hot girls in the background too. The hours on set might be ridiculously long but Justin knows that by the end they will have a really polished, slick video that his fans will love. He can never pick one song out when people ask him which of his own records he likes the best because he loves them all for different reasons. He has very fond memories of filming his old YouTube videos back in Stratford with his mum.

For 'One Time', Justin's first video, they decided to shoot it in Usher's house rather than renting a luxury house somewhere else. This made it more authentic because the house in the video was supposed to be Usher's house. Justin wanted his best friend Ryan to be in the video so they flew him to Atlanta. At the start of the video Ryan and Justin played video games like they always did, but they were being filmed. It was an amazing experience for both Justin and Ryan, and they got to share it together.

Justin loves the buzz that goes with releasing a single and hearing what his fans think of it. His first single 'One Time' started being played on the radio from 18 May 2009 and fans in the USA and Canada could buy it from 7 July 2009. It wasn't released in the UK until 4 January 2010. His second single 'One Less Lonely Girl' was released in the USA and Canada initially through iTunes only on 6 October 2009. 2010 saw the release of 'Baby' in the USA and Canada on 18 January and in the UK on 7 March. Next up was a remix of 'Somebody to Love' featuring Usher which was released on 25 June and 'U Smile' came out on 24 August.

When his first single 'One Time' was released he talked to Digital Spy about what the song was about: "'One Time' is basically about being in a typical teen relationship so it's a song everyone can relate to. You know when you're younger and you thought it was love, but then later on you realise it was just puppy love? That's what the song's about."

He has to do so much promotional work whenever he is releasing a single or an album but he always smiles and gets on with it because he feels blessed to have the opportunity to release his music all around the world.

Style

Every great pop star needs a great stylist and for Justin this person is Ryan Good. He has been with Justin since he first started out and was also his road manager for a bit. They are good friends and Ryan is always 100 per cent honest with Justin. When Justin started promoting his first singles around the USA, Ryan would travel with him and look after him. Justin always has his mum with him but it helped having Ryan too because he knew all about the music business.

During an interview with *T* magazine Justin was asked about his style and what he splurges on. He told them: "I don't actually spend a lot of money… I'm not a splurger, but I like clothes like G-star and I really like shoes, I wear Supers a lot. I wear a lot of hoodies, but I also like Alexander McQueen. I think he is very original and does amazing stuff."

Justin definitely has more shoes than a normal teenage boy, as he has sneakers in so many different colours. He likes to make a statement with his footwear. Ryan is Justin's swagger coach as well as his stylist. This confuses some people because they don't understand what a swagger coach is. Justin explained to Macleans.ca: "It's pretty simple... he kind of teaches me, he helps me just stay swaggerific. I don't know."

To Justin 'swaggerific' means having lots of confidence in the way you move and your style.

When Justin is taking part in magazine photo shoots the stylists can pick out horrible clothes for him to wear. He often doesn't have the luxury of picking out his own outfit with Ryan. Normally Justin is quite open to trying something new but sometimes he has to put his foot down. He told *Top of the Pops* magazine: "Well, I try not to be rude, but people push and push you. I was at this photo shoot and these guys were like, 'Put this on, it looks really cool,' and I was like, 'I don't really like that, I don't wanna wear that.' This is me, I wear a hoodie, I'm just easy."

T is for...

Talent Competition

When Justin was 12 he entered The Stratford Star talent competition. The first prize was a microphone and a session in a recording studio. Justin wanted the chance to perform in front of people and if he won it would be a bonus. He just wanted to have some fun. He paid two dollars to enter – and he's so glad he did now when he looks back.

The competition took place over four weeks at the Kiwanis Community Centre.

For the first round Justin sang '3 AM' by Matchbox 20. He impressed the judges and the audience and made it through to round two. He then decided to sing Alicia Keys's 'Fallin'. The audience loved it even more and he sailed through to round three. He picked Aretha Franklin's 'Respect' next, and managed to do enough to get into the final.

Justin was super confident when he performed 'Respect'. He danced around the stage, chanted "Come on" in between the lines and played an invisible saxophone along with the music. The only thing that went wrong was that he dropped the microphone at one point in the performance, but he just picked it up and carried on.

In the final Justin had to sing twice. He picked 'So Sick' by Ne-Yo and 'Basketball' by Lil' Bow Wow. Each song showed off Justin's voice in a different way. The audience loved his performances and the judges did too, placing him in the top three!

Justin was a lot younger than the other finalists and hadn't even performed in public before round one but it still hurt when his name wasn't called out as the winner. He didn't let anyone see how hurt he was and instead congratulated Kristen Hawley for winning. He had gone from feeling on top of the world to feeling terrible... but it wasn't the end. His mum wanted to show their friends and family members who hadn't been able to be there how great Justin had sang so she decided to put the videos of the rounds on YouTube.

For a long time Justin thought he had finished in second place on that day but in actual fact he finished in third. They never announced who came runner-up but the woman who counted up the votes revealed it to the press once Justin was famous.

Mimi Price who played a big part in the organisation of the show told *The Star*: "We knew there was something special, but we thought 'Give him a couple years with voice training and he would have the whole package.' He was definitely up for the challenge and he had the charisma, he just didn't have the experience."

Justin doesn't hold anything against the judges for not naming him the winner and has been back to the community centre since. Mimi knows Justin's life has changed but he will always be that boy from the competition to her. She told the paper: "When he walked in at Christmas [2009], he had a BlackBerry in one hand and a credit card in the other. He was going to pay for his [$4] day fee to come in. I said 'It's okay, Justin, it's on us. What's with the credit card? He said: 'I'm travelling.'"

DID YOU KNOW?

Justin used to go to a nursery in the same building where the competition was held.

Tattoo

When news broke in May 2010 that Justin had gotten a tattoo most of his fans were shocked because he was so young and he hadn't told them about it. He had actually had the tattoo for two months when photographers snapped him playing on the beach in Australia without a shirt on. The tattoo is tiny and sits on his hip.

Justin went with his dad to get the tattoo done at the Son Of A Gun Tattoo and Barber Shop. The owner of the shop is an old friend of Justin's dad. Brian Byrne told MTV: "It was a 16th birthday tattoo... I guess his dad has it, and one of his uncles. It's the outline of the seagull from Jonathan Livingston Seagull."

Justin was only allowed to have the tattoo done because he was with his dad as you have to be with a parent until you are 18, and he was only 16.

Brian didn't say a word to the press until the news broke because he wanted to respect Justin's privacy. It's not known if Justin will have any more tattoos in the

future. His dad has at least five tattoos on his arm, chest, hip and stomach.

If you haven't seen Justin's tattoo or the photo of him getting it done then just Google 'Justin Bieber tattoo'. Maybe his baby brother Jaxon will get the same tattoo when he is 16… we'll just have to wait and see.

Touring

Justin experienced what having a tour would be like back in early 2009. The Canadian clothing retailer Urban Behavior asked whether he would be interested in doing a mini-tour and he jumped at the chance. The tour was due to kick off in the Urban Behavior store in Vancouver on 1 November and then go to the Edmonton, Montreal, London (the Canadian city) and Toronto stores. At each location Justin would sign Urban Behavior t-shirts, pose for photos and chat to fans.

Justin ended up missing the first date because he was ill so the staff at the Vancouver Urban Behavior store gave the disappointed fans a special discount and encouraged them to sign a Get Well Soon card for Justin. Thankfully he didn't have to cancel any of the other dates and so many fans turned up to see him. He thanked them all on Twitter and admitted that he was surprised.

The best and worst day of the mini-tour was probably Toronto. It was the last day of the tour and Justin must have been gutted that it was the end but at the same time he got to perform at the club Kool Haus after he had finished at the Urban Behavior store which was really cool. As he performed on stage the fans watching started to scream and chant "We love you, Justin!"

Justin didn't just sing a couple of quick songs, he really gave it his all. He performed 'Bigger', 'One Less Lonely Girl', an acoustic version of 'Favourite Girl' and ended with Chris Brown's 'With You'. He told the people watching: "This has been like a cool rollercoaster ride... thanks to crowds like you guys."

Justin loved his mini-tour and it made him want to go on a proper tour as soon as possible. He had loved meeting fans and signing autographs but he wanted to perform onstage in front of thousands of people. He was so excited when he found out the My World tour was going to happen. It had dates in 85 cities in the USA and Canada... and the first one was at Hartford, Connecticut on 23th June.

Justin left Stratford a couple of days before the first show so he had time to rehearse and prepare. All performers find the week leading up to their tour a bit strange as they want to get on and perform. Justin knew his family and friends would all be in the audience on the first night so he had to make sure he gave it his all.

He tweeted on 21th June: "Canada thank u!! Sad I had 2 leave but we r starting the tour and had to get back to rehearsals....MY BUS RULES!! It's a party on wheels!"

Justin has had so many surprise guests join him on stage during his tour. These included Miley Cyrus, Usher, Akon, Bow Wow, Boyz II Men and Jaden Smith. Justin loved seeing his fans' reactions when they saw who the special guest was.

In 2011 there were no USA or Canada dates planned. Instead Justin would be travelling to Europe, Asia and Australia. He had a break of three months to start with before touring the UK and Ireland from 4th March to 24th March. He then had dates in Germany, The Netherlands, France, Belgium, Denmark, Germany, Spain, Switzerland, Italy, Israel and Indonesia lined up before heading over to Australia from 26th April to 26th May. He then had more dates in Asia from 10th May to 19th May before finishing the tour on 21st May in Brazil (his only date in South America).

In 2010 Justin's family went on tour with him – his grandparents, his mum all wanted to be there for him and witness him on stage having the time of his life. His dog even came along some of the time. For his 2011 dates his mum would still be there but his wider family wouldn't be able to go to as many performances as they had done the year before because they were so far away from Stratford.

Justin had to work out quite a bit before the tour started to make sure that he had what it takes to put on a big show for 75 minutes. He needed to build his body up so it would be able to handle it. By the time the My World tour finishes Justin will have been touring for almost a full year, and he will be so used to his exercise regime and schedule that it might be weird for him when things go back to normal. His last date will no doubt be sad for Justin as he will have to say goodbye to some of his crew. He feels like they are one big family. At least they will be able to reunite when Justin starts his second big tour – although no set plans have been made it is probably going to happen in 2012, as his first tour has been such a success to date.

DID YOU KNOW?

Justin never normally gets nervous before he goes on stage but when it came to the day of his opening night in Hartford he was feeling the pressure. It seemed like every magazine and website was waiting to see how Justin did on his first night and his fans had been talking about how good it was going to be for months.

He tweeted just before he went on stage: "Sorry been away all day…first tour ever. Little nervous. Don't want to let u guys down."

Justin might have been nervous on the inside but he didn't look it at all as he belted out his biggest hits and put on the most amazing show his fans had ever seen.

Afterwards he tweeted: "2nite was just…well…i was scared. didnt want to let anyone down but the energy and the fans were incredible. Cant wait to do this again!"

Justin's fans who have seen the show already and have left amazing reviews on ticket sites, websites and blogs.

One fan going by the name JBieberLover on ticketmaster.com wrote: "The Justin Bieber concert was amazing! It was my very 1st concert and I think if I go to another concert I will have high expectations because this one was so good! Of course Justin was amazing, but the show was too. The lasers and the hovering objects Justin sat in were really cool. It got the crowd hyped! I loved the show and I hope he comes to my town again!

"My favorite moment was when Justin got into the

floating heart and sang Never Let you Go and Favorite Girl acoustically."

Another fan OliviaLol agreed: "Best concert ever! Justin Bieber is a good singer. I sat on the floor seats. Jasmine V was ok. But Sean Kingston really got me and the crowd pumped up! The opening of the concert was awesome! He sang 'Love Me'. Sometime during the concert he showed a preview of his new movie *Never Say Never*. He also introduced his band. Justin did a cover of 'Wanna Be Starting Something' by Michael Jackson. He sung his hit songs which was good. The final song was 'Baby' and in the end confetti came out! I have to say this is the BEST concert EVER!"

The press have given mixed reviews of Justin's tour performances but most agree that Justin's fans enjoy every second of his show.

Tour Facts

- Nine lorries are used to transport Justin's set and equipment to the next venue
- He has such a big crew that they need 11 tour buses (Justin's is the nicest)
- Each night, one million pieces of confetti are used

JUSTIN PERFORMS IN TIMES SQUARE IN 2009.

- Justin chills out behind the scenes playing on his Xbox – he loves these three games the most: 'Call of Duty: Modern Warfare', 'NBA2K10, and 'Madden'.

When Justin is on tour he has an amazing time but he can get homesick. He doesn't get much time off so he can't go home that often. To combat this he pays for flights for the people he is missing to come and see him.

His dad really misses him when he is away but he has two small children at home so he couldn't go on tour with Justin every day like his mum does. He just hops on a plane to where Justin is whenever he can and Justin will no doubt visit him lots once the tour finishes.

Twitter

Justin wouldn't have such a good relationship with his fans if it wasn't for Twitter. He loves being able to send messages to his fans, and hearing what they have to say. Justin is arguably the best celebrity on Twitter as he follows way more fans than other celebrities. As of January 2011, he was following a humungous 102,531 people!

Forbes.com actually named Justin as the most influential Twitter celebrity of 2011 after they ranked celebrities according to their 'social media influence'. They looked at how many followers the celebrities had and how many people had retweeted their messages and linked back. Interaction between the celebrity and their fans was important. Lady Gaga might have more followers than Justin but her score wasn't as high. She only managed to get 89.6 points which left her in seventh place.

The higher the score was on the 'Klout' scale the more influential the celebrity. Justin achieved the maximum score of 100 followed by author Paul Coelho, who wrote *The Alchemist*, with 96. Nick Jonas was third with a score of 92 followed by Kanye West in fourth with a score of 90.9.

Justin might have millions of fans but he never takes them for granted. He values each person for supporting him and would thank them all individually if he could. When he found out that he had reached 6 million fans on Twitter on 9 November he was so overwhelmed. He tweeted: "6 MILLION OF THE GREATEST FANS ON EARTH ON TWITTER!!!! THANK U. This is crazy... My Hometown only has 30,000 people total! NUTS

He carried on: "so let me break this down for you...this is for all the kids out there with a dream.... for every person out there who gets told you cant be somebody or achieve something. for everyone who dreams of something more...

"im from a small town many have never heard of...my parents had me as teenagers...me and my mom lived in a small apartment... no one in my family had really left my town or the area and i never thought leaving was possible….but then u all found me…. and you all changed my life and showed me opportunity i didnt think existed. you taught me to #dreambig and #neversaynever. so thank u."

Fans felt inspired by these messages and thousands retweeted them. Who knows what Justin will say when he reaches 7 million followers soon. Knowing how popular he is he'll probably achieve 8 million followers by the end of 2011.

Some people have suggested that Justin actually uses 3 per cent of Twitter's servers at any given time but Twitter have neither denied nor admitted that this is the case. The rumours started when a web designer called Dustin Curtis tweeted: "At any moment, Justin Bieber uses 3% of our infrastructure. Racks of servers are dedicated to him. – A guy who works at Twitter"

A Twitter spokesperson told Mashable when asked whether they were confirming if it was true: "While we don't break out metrics like this, everything around and about Justin Bieber is consistently popular on Twitter."

Mashable seem to think that Dustin Curtis and his source may be right when you consider: "Every time Bieber tweets, his messages have to be delivered to more than five million people who then endlessly retweet it. Apparently, his account receives more than 60 @-replies per second for a while after he tweets, which is something Twitter wasn't originally designed to handle."

If Justin does take up 3 per cent of Twitter's servers sometimes then it's no wonder that when he tweeted that he found the MTV show *The Hard Times of RJ Berger* funny, ratings for the show went up. Apparently 9 per cent more people tuned in for the next episode and the following week ratings had gone up by 14 per cent. When the announcement was made that there was going to be a second series some people thought it was down to Justin.

It seems like Justin has so much influence but in reality fans might try a show Justin recommends but if they don't like it they'll switch over. Also Justin appeals to so many different types of people that his Twitter followers have different likes, dislikes, dreams and ambitions. They might be 5 or they might be 65 years old.

When journalist Nicholas Kohler was interviewing Justin for Macleans.ca, Justin talked to him about how important social networking is. He said: "[Being on Twitter, Facebook, YouTube] is something that is very good for any new artist. I think that the Internet is something that keeps your fans involved in the project. They can talk to you, they can write to you, you're able to interact with your fans, you can keep them updated,

you can put videos on YouTube saying where you are, and it just makes them feel like they're part of the project. It's a new day and age. I think a lot of older artists didn't have the chance to use the Internet and Facebook. It's a great way to bring your fans in."

Justin wouldn't be able to be the artist he is today without Twitter and he couldn't imagine not having the ability to tweet his followers his latest news. That is why he always takes his laptop and mobile wherever he goes so he can post up pictures and messages. Other celebrities have decided to delete their Twitter accounts, leaving some fans upset and hurt. Miley Cyrus, John Mayer and Demi Lovato are just three celebrities who left millions of fans behind when they decided not to tweet any more.

U is for...

UK

Justin's UK fans might have had to wait longer than his American and Canadian fans to get hold of his music but they are just as dedicated. They arranged a parade in London on 25th October 2010 to show Justin how much they loved him and needed him to come back to the UK as he hadn't been over since Capital's Summertime Ball on 6th June, and they missed him loads. Around 200 fans took part in the parade organised by superfans Hasti and Gulcan. The girls run a site called Justin Bieber London and they always keep track of when he is in the UK so that Justin's UK fans don't miss out. They were desperate for him to announce a UK tour and that was what the fans who took part were trying to achieve.

Less than three weeks later Justin announced via Twitter that he would be touring the UK in 2011. All the fans who took part in the march were delighted that Justin would be performing his concert in Liverpool, Manchester, Birmingham, Newcastle, Sheffield, Nottingham and of course London. They had dreamt that it might happen but for Justin to do so many dates was amazing.

Justin was also looking forward to performing for his Irish fans in Dublin.

It would be nice if Justin had some time off to explore the UK because there is so much to see. It would be cool if he went to Stratford-upon-Avon because his hometown of Stratford was named after Shakespeare's birthplace and it has many similarities to the town.

Justin could never live in the UK permanently because of the weather. He told Fearne Cotton on Radio 1: "I couldn't live here because the weather's depressing. Very depressing. But I like the girls!"

He has tried to do an English accent before in an interview but ended up sounding Australian. Maybe he should get himself an English girlfriend to teach him how to do it right... any volunteers?

Usher

Usher is a hugely successful singer, producer and businessman. He has sold over 45 million records and has 5 Grammys under his belt. He is Justin's mentor and best showbiz buddy. He has helped Justin so much and will always be there for his 'little bro'. Seeing Justin become the huge star he is today has made Usher so happy.

When Usher started to mentor Justin he guided him in the way he should go. Justin was completely new to the music business and needed as much advice as Usher could give him. Justin reeled off what he was told on *The Today Show*: "stay humble, stay grounded, remember where you come from, family is really important and don't forget that."

Usher was the same age as Justin when he started out but he didn't have instant success and it took him until his second album *My Way* came out in 1997 to gain the recognition he deserved. Usher told the *New York Times*: "I understand the pressure to be in that position... But I had a chance to ramp up my success, where this has happened to him abruptly. So Scooter, Ryan, myself: we tag-team him."

Usher told MTV in April 2010: "You haven't seen the best of him. He is a pop craze like The Beatles. They started out as pure pop artists and look what they became over the years.

USHER HAS BEEN ONE OF THE MOST IMPORTANT PEOPLE IN JUSTIN'S CAREER SO FAR.

"Justin reminds me of myself at that age, only he's a much more talented musician than I was. He taught himself piano and guitar. I couldn't, so he has that advantage."

Usher has even gone as far as to say that he thinks that Justin will achieve more than he has done in his career – and to beat five Grammys would be hard for anyone but Justin. Justin will probably have a room full of Grammys by the time he's 30. Usher is so proud of him and wants the world to know it. He talked to the *Los Angeles Times* about what impressed him about Justin. Usher said: "I think it was, first and foremost, his charming, winning, timeless attitude. When I met him, his personality won me over. When he sang, I realized we were dealing with the real thing.

"His voice just spoke to the type of music I would want to be associated with. And it wasn't a gimmick – we had to teach him how to dance and be on stage, but he really had a good voice."

Usher knows that Justin is just at the start of his career and that he is going to become an even bigger global superstar. He will always be there for Justin, guiding him and helping him the best way he can. Justin is just grateful that Usher wanted to mentor him and appreciates the fact that he can call him any time, day or night, if he has a problem or something is troubling him.

V is for...

Virginity

It is thought that Justin wants to keep his virginity until he gets married. He doesn't talk about it or wear a purity ring like Miley Cyrus and the Jonas Brothers do but according to his mum he has told her he wants to stay pure.

MTV reports that Pattie said: "He's expressed his desire to stay pure, and honour women, and treat women with respect. So hopefully that stays valid."

Justin knows he will meet the right girl one day to be Mrs Bieber. Justin's fans are going to be so gutted for themselves but happy for him at the same time when he does.

Vocal Coach

Justin's vocal coach is called Jan Smith and she is one of the best in the business. Her nickname is Mama Jan. She is the person who is helping Justin adjust as he is going through puberty. She also helped Usher when he faced the same issues with his voice, over 15 years ago.

The fact that their voice is changing stresses most boys out who are Justin's age because they don't know what their voice will be like: they know it will be deeper but they don't know how deep. For a singer it is even tougher because their voice is everything; if they can't sing then it's the end of the road for them.

Mama Jan must have really put Justin's mind at rest because he told *OK* magazine back in July 2010: "Everyone's voice changes, puberty is a natural thing.

"I have the best vocal coach in the world and we're working on my voice and doing what I need to do. It's not like as soon as you hit puberty you stop singing."

Only a few months earlier Justin had admitted that he was unable to reach the high notes in 'Baby' and he now has to do it in a lower key. Fans don't mind though because he sounds amazing whatever key he sings in.

Jan has taught Justin so much because he couldn't afford singing lessons when he was growing up so she had to teach him from scratch. People think that singing is easy, you just open your mouth and the right sound comes out but it's not that simple. Singers have to train their voices and it takes hours of practising every day for singers to 'tune their instrument.' Justin had raw talent but he needed Jan's help to become the world class singer he is today. He had to have a lot of lessons with Jan before he was ready even to set foot in a recording studio, let alone record anything.

W is for...

Willow Smith

Willow is the daughter of Will Smith and his wife Jada Pinkett-Smith. She has two older brothers, Trey and Jaden. Jaden sang on 'Never Say Never' with Justin and played the lead role in *The Karate Kid*. The whole Smith family have been good friends of Justin and his mum for quite a while.

Willow is an actress and a singer. Her first single 'Whip My Hair' was a big hit around the world ending up at number 11 in the USA Charts and number 2 in the UK. Justin loved it when Willow appeared as a special guest during his concert at the Staples Centre in Los Angeles on 25th October.

WILLOW AND HER BROTHER JADEN ARE REALLY GOOD FRIENDS WITH JUSTIN.

She can dance as well as sing and had a bit of a dance-off with Justin on stage as they tried to teach the audience how to do the Dougie.

He was so happy when he found out that she would be supporting him on tour in 2011. She was, too, and tweeted: "Got news that my big bro @justinbieber invited me on his European Tour in March..so exciting! Maybe I'll let Jaden come..LOL #NEVERSAYNEVER"

Justin retweeted her message and then sent this message back: "@OfficialWillow get ready…i got more surprises coming. #MYWORLDTOUR."

Having Willow and her family on tour with him will really help Justin feel less homesick. Willow's mum Jada will be nice company for Pattie too because Justin's crew is mainly made up of men.

X is for...

X Factor

Justin's biggest TV appearance in the UK to date was on *The X Factor*. He performed a mash-up of 'Somebody to Love' and 'Baby' on the results show on 28th November. He wore a black leather jacket with a big Stratford badge on it – his friends and family from home must have loved the not-so-subtle shout out to them. Justin's UK fans had been waiting a long time to see him on the *X Factor* stage.

When host Dermot O'Leary asked Justin if he was nervous performing in front of Simon Cowell, he replied: "I wasn't that nervous, I was pretty cool, pretty calm, pretty collected."

X Factor judge, Cheryl Cole.

Justin doesn't get nervous when he's performing and he had already met Simon when he performed on *American Idol* so he knew he had nothing to worry about. He was more interested in meeting Cheryl Cole. He told Dermot: "I want to say hello to Cheryl Cole, hello." He smiled at Cheryl and held his hand up to his ear as if it was a phone. He wanted her to call him so they could go on a date.

Simon Cowell really likes Justin and might use him in the USA version of *The X Factor* when he launches it later in 2011. Simon told Extra TV: "He put himself forward to judge some of the episodes."

DID YOU KNOW?

Justin has offered to give Zayn from *X Factor* band One Direction some dancing lessons. They had a chat backstage.

Y is for...

YouTube

It's scary to think that if Justin's mum hadn't decided to post videos up on YouTube for his friends and family to see then Justin might have never been discovered. Justin might have tried out for *American Idol* once he was old enough but we would have missed out on all the great music he has been producing for the last two years.

Justin's username on YouTube is 'Kidrauhl.' Many fans wonder why he picked that name but it is all because of his dad. His dad uses the name Lordrauhl on YouTube and he used to use it when he played an online card game called Spades. The website Jeremy used to go on to play has closed down now but a few years ago Lordrauhl was one of the site's best players. He wrote on his website back then: "I got the name lordrauhl from a series of books I read (the main character being Lord Rahl).

"I've been playing this style of spades for approximately five years now, and I consider myself one of the elite players at playsite. Part of my game... is getting you off yours."

Lord Rauhl is a character from *The Sword of Truth* series by Terry Goodkind. They are epic fantasy novels and there are 11 books in the series. Jeremy must really love them because he has kept using Lordrauhl as his online name. In choosing the username Kidrauhl Justin is paying tribute to his dad and in many ways is saying 'Son of Jeremy'.

If you haven't checked out Justin's or his dad's YouTube channels then you really need to. On the Lordrauhl channel you can see videos of Justin playing basketball with his dad, his dad fishing, and videos of Justin's little brother and sister playing. It is nice that Jeremy is willing to share these videos with Justin's fans.

The Kidrauhl channel has so many videos of Justin performing for you to watch, backstage videos, personal videos where Justin chats to his fans, videos of him with Usher and Sean Kingston... if you haven't seen them yet then you are definitely missing out.

Lots of fans have been visiting Justin's channel and checking out his official videos. Fans have also been posting up their own fan videos of Justin and there are lots of video interviews on YouTube of Justin on TV programmes around the world.

When YouTube released its Top Ten Most Viewed Music Videos of 2010 Justin must have been ecstatic. Four of his videos made the list and 'Baby' was at number one with 406 million views. That is crazy! Here is the full list:

1. 'Baby' by Justin Bieber, 406 million views
2. 'Waka Waka' by Shakira, 254 million views
3. 'Love the Way You Lie' by Eminem, 229 million views
4. 'Not Afraid' by Eminem, 164 million views
5. 'Rude Boy' by Rihanna, 118 million views
6. 'Never Say Never' by Justin Bieber, 118 million views
7. 'Never Let You Go', by Justin Bieber, 108 million views
8. 'Alejandro' by Lady Gaga, 108 million views
9. 'Somebody To Love' by Justin Bieber, 103 million views
10. 'Telephone' by Lady Gaga, 95 million views

Everyone is certain that Justin will have even more success in 2011 so he might have six or seven videos in YouTube's Top Ten.

Z is for...

Zone

Before every performance Justin needs to get in the zone. He can't just rush on stage, he needs to sit and prepare himself for what he is about to do. Some performers like listening to music before they go on stage, other performers like to move around and psych themselves up. Beyoncé Knowles actually pretends to be a person called Sasha Fierce to perform. Justin likes to pray with his mum and his crew. He focuses on God and then goes and does his performance.

Another zone that is connected to our favourite guy is the Justin Bieber Zone website. It is the biggest Justin

Bieber fan site in the world. Check it out for yourself if you haven't already: www.justinbieberzone.com.

On it you will find the latest news stories, photos, lyrics to Justin's songs, information on tour tickets, videos and forums. It is run by Durian, Zuhri and Michelle and was launched on 30 October 2009.

HERE IS A LIST OF MORE GREAT FAN SITES YOU MIGHT WANT TO CHECK OUT:

J-Bieber.org
Justinbieberfan.org
Ultimatebieber.org
Justinbieber.bz

If you are hungry for more, head over to Justin's Official website – www.justinbiebermusic.com